Cinched

Living with *Unwavering Trust* in an *Unfailing God*

Look who recommends *Cinched.*

"In *Cinched: Living with Unwavering Trust in an Unfailing God*, Kristine's message of how to trust God is dripping with truth from God's Word that will not only encourage your heart, but challenge it. It's both biblical and beautiful. You'll be left with no choice but to cling to the only One who can truly help in time of need. A down to earth encouraging read for a struggling heart."

— MICAH MADDOX, Women's Event Speaker,
and Author of *Anchored In: Experience a Power-Full
Life in a Problem-Filled World*

"Do I live like I trust God? That's the key question Kristine Brown explores that is a foundational question for every believer in God. Can what we say we believe about God be lived out in word and deed with trusting obedience? I'm good at saying I trust God but even as I read *Cinched*, I had to face that I was not living in trust in God in a current situation. That's why I believe every Christian needs Kristine's book. There are always new layers within our hearts, minds, and souls that require new steps of deeper trust. And what better biblical woman could Kristine choose to help us than Rahab, who faced real danger yet took steps of faith. *Cinched* is an inspiring book with real life examples, deep biblical truths, and a focus on God's character which is an essential element for me. I highly recommend this empowering book.

—KATHY COLLARD MILLER, international speaker and
author of many books including *God's Intriguing Questions.*
www.KathyCollardMiller.com

"If you find yourself waking up to worry on your mind instead of trust in your heart for a God in control, this book is for you. Kristine Brown writes in a come-alongside manner about how she learned to trust God and find peace on her journey, even when the circumstances were hard. Through personal stories and biblical insights, Brown's words supply exactly what's needed to move from doubt in the unknowns of life to trust in an unwavering God."

— **GAYLA GRACE**, Staff Writer and Speaker for
FamilyLife®, author of *Stepparenting with Grace.*

"Her words fuel a beautifully deep trust in Christ, even in hard times. Her life displays this message, too. Using her own story and Rahab's, Kristine Brown champions women like us to forgo the struggle and live a life steeped with trust in God instead. So grab a cup of tea and settle in. This might be the tool to help you find that courage you've been searching for all along."

— **KRISTI WOODS**, Storyteller of God's Glory through
Christian Romance & Nonfiction at *KristiWoods.net*

"How do we live with hope when everything around us points to disaster? Kristine Brown skillfully answers that question with the ancient story of Rahab, interwoven with her own personal battle that required full trust in God. It's a combination that will inspire and help you to claim hope for yourself, no matter what comes along. Are you struggling to trust God? Then this is the book for you!"

— **JULIE ZINE COLEMAN**, Author of *Unexpected Love:
God's Heart Revealed through Jesus' Conversations with Women*
and *On Purpose: Understanding God's Freedom
for Women through Scripture* (releasing 2.22.22)
and managing editor at *AriseDaily.com.*

"My friend and I often laugh at the phrase "expectation versus reality". Kristine invites us to forgo expectation and simply trust God. Kristine Brown's transparency sharing her personal story coupled with faith offered by an unlikely heroine, Rahab, encourage and uplift. Reading *Cinched* inspired me to hold fast to God's promises. I might just hang a scarlet cord out of my window."

— **AMY PRIDDY**, Ministry wife and Author of
Journaling through the Old Testament &
Journaling through the New Testament

"We know bold faith is the hallmark of a Christian walk, and we want it, but when life hits hard, we find our faith wilting. How do we walk in steadfast faith no matter what? In *Cinched*, Kristine Brown masterfully weaves the story of Rahab's brave faith with her own experience learning to actively trust God through her difficult cancer journey. While tight-fisting our circumstances only leads to what-ifs and worst-case scenarios, Kristine offers a series of foundational principles showing how to trust God at the deepest level—in our decisions, relationships, and long waits. *Cinched* is the galvanizing study we need to tether our trust to God."

— **LISA APPELO,** Author of *Life Can Be Good Again: Putting Your World Back Together After It All Falls Apart* (releasing April, 2022)

Cinched

Living with *Unwavering Trust* in an *Unfailing God*

KRISTINE BROWN

Aberdeen
BOOKS LLC

ISBN: 978-1-7375986-0-2

Library of Congress Control Number: 2021914969
Library of Congress Cataloging-in-Publication Data has been requested.

Cover & Interior Design by: Five J's Design
Editing Services by: Five J's Design
Author Photo by: Tilmon Photography

In memory of Tonya and George for showing me how to trust God through it all.

Table of Contents

Do I Live Like I Trust God?

I ran my finger along the seal, knowing the diagnosis scribbled in doctor's handwriting hid just beneath the stark white fold. Even the light streaming from the window couldn't give away its secret. Bullying thoughts urged me to just get it over with, to slip my finger under the edge and lift. Satisfy what I'd been dreading. But I knew what would happen once I read those words.

I knew.

Because I'd been there before, receiving devastating news and being completely unraveled. I knew if I chose to open the envelope, I'd become vulnerable to the words written in bold black ink. Once sealed in the folder marked "permanent file" in my mind, those words would gain more power than they deserved.

It had only been a few short weeks since I made it through the last battle. I'd held on for dear life. To what? I don't know. I just prayed for the strength to get through it, each day hoping for relief. Now instead of getting the reprieve I longed for, I came face-to-face with something even worse. And with it, a thought wrapped in one life-defining question.

"Do I live like I trust God to handle this?"

It should've shocked me. The question, I mean. If you were to look at my life today, you'd probably say, "Of course someone like her trusts God!" I pray. I have my daily devotional time. I read the Bible and even memorize verses. Yet instead of exuding peace, joy, and victorious living, I live in a perpetual state of defeat. When decisions must be made, my kids don't have it all together, or I face a mountain of challenges.

Yes, the answer to my question "Do I live like I trust God to handle this?" came all too easily. And with it, knowing something had to change. Not in my circumstances, but in how I *walked through* my circumstances.

I felt the weight of the envelope grow heavier every second. I could allow its contents to drive me back into a pattern of worry, frustration, and doubt, or I could take a step toward discovering peace. Would I choose to move to a new level of trust in the God I claimed to know?

That choice would mean pressing beyond knowing and saying to actually doing. Truth be told, I'd been stuck. Stuck rehashing the same problem. Stuck beneath a mound of crippling thoughts. Stuck fearing the worst or wondering how things could possibly work out. Until the envelope, I hadn't uncovered the real issue.

"No, I didn't live like I trusted God."

I glared at it again, this time with new resolve. I wouldn't open it until I knew without a doubt that, whatever it said, I would trust God without wavering. I needed to believe, whether the doctor wrote, "stage 1, 2, 3, or 4," God would take care of me. No matter what. I wouldn't just say it; I'd live it.

I whispered, "Okay Lord, you've got this." I tucked the unopened envelope back in the pocket of my three-ring binder and closed it.

The few moments holding that sealed envelope became a turning point in my life. One that sparked a deep desire for change. Maybe you sense it too, right now as you read these words. The desire to do things differently this time, or the realization that you can't endure one more hard thing, not the way you have been. But there is hope.

We're not alone in our yearning to live in the victory that comes with steadfast faith. Because the truth is, our ability to trust God affects every part of our lives, including our decisions, relationships, and how we handle difficult circumstances. Yes, we want to trust God in all things, but time and again we falter instead of agreeing with what we know to be true. That is the essence of this book: to feel frustration, doubt, and indecision loosen their hold as we learn to secure our faith to God's promises.

But before we join hands and move forward together—sisters linked with a shared vision for a life filled with newfound trust—we need to do one quick thing. We need to prepare our hearts for all God has in store.

What to Expect When You're Not Expecting

You may have picked up this book because, like me, you love a good story. Especially if that story includes a fierce woman from the Bible. Maybe you joined a study group to read it with friends. Or maybe—just maybe—you scanned the back cover and felt a tugging at your heart that would not let go because you've been there.

- Wondering why a prayer-answering God didn't answer yours.

- Thinking if only you'd done something differently, things wouldn't be so bad right now.

- Waking up with worry on your mind instead of praise to the One you know is in control.

- Frustrated with the lousy decisions your loved ones keep making.

- Losing sleep as you overanalyze every possible outcome of the opportunity before you.

- Overwhelmed with the uncertainty of it all.

Whatever prompted you to pick up this book, would you do me a favor as a friend? Release every expectation of what you thought you would gain from it. Let it go.

Expectations can be a good thing. Leading a small group at work, directing a women's Bible study, and even being a mom all require us to set expectations and help the people in our lives work toward those goals. But I've learned loosening our grip opens our hearts to new possibilities. (You can trust me on this. I struggle with grip-loosening.)

I've been known to hold some high expectations. Some might even say unrealistic. Just ask my kids! When we hold on to an expectation, we tend to give that our focus. If you're a go-getter girl like me, you might even fixate on it. (Can I get a witness?) And I don't want you to miss out on anything God has planned for you. Let's do this together. Are you ready? Here goes…

> *"I am releasing my expectations and opening my heart to
> let God speak to me as I read this book."*

I believe in making promises. Not just any promises, but ones stacked firmly in God's Word. Because if there is one thing I am most certain of, it is this: God keeps His promises. Every. Single. Time. We will explore a lot about that in the chapters ahead, so thank you for allowing me to start with a bold proclamation right from the beginning. We will discover truth in the pages ahead—proof of the power of God's guarantee—through my story of learning to trust God thanks to a woman who has inspired multitudes. A woman named Rahab. We will immerse ourselves in Rahab's story as if we are right there with this gutsy woman from Scripture. Thanks to her testimony, I'll offer guiding principles gleaned from Rahab's life to help us turn out-of-control thoughts into trusting Him like we mean it.

When I began writing this book, people would ask me the question that causes authors to either panic or freeze.

"So, what's your book about?"

Seems like an easy task to answer such a simple question, especially when you've been getting to live out the topic for months or even years. But I get tongue-tied the instant I see the question coming. I blurt out the simplest response, saving me from ensuing rapid heartbeat or breaking out in hives.

"It's a book about Rahab."

Only, there's a serious problem with that answer. It isn't true. This is *not* a book about Rahab, or me, or you, or any one person or one victory.

It's *for* every woman who has ever struggled to trust God, whether in her daily decisions, her relationships with family and friends, or when life gets scary and hard. It's for discovering the peace, resolve, and victorious living that come from trusting a God who cannot fail. So, why wait another second? Let's begin our move to a Rahab-level of trust. I'm beyond grateful you chose to join me.

CHAPTER 1

Preparing to Weave
a New Cord

TRUSTING GOD LIKE WE MEAN IT.

*"They will have no fear of bad news;
their hearts are steadfast, trusting in the Lord."*

PSALM 112:7 NIV

Tomorrow a woman we know will wake up rehashing the same problem she prayed about yesterday. She will begin the day agonizing over how in the world it could possibly work out. The cycle will repeat. Agonizing will turn to complaining, then to doubt, until she returns to church Sunday, where she will slouch in defeat, realizing she spent the whole week worrying about something she thought she gave to God.

She knows God is real. She reads Scripture, tells Him her problems, and even says she trusts Him with the outcomes. She pauses for daily devotions and even recalls several Bible verses by heart. She prays for her family and remembers to "cast her cares on Him," knowing that's what God wants her to do. Yet her actions don't reflect this knowledge she has of who God is. She still lives with frustration, sleepless nights, and stress-filled days.

Does this sound familiar? I hope so, because I'd hate to think I'm the only one. Strength in numbers and all that. You see, *I am* that woman, from my now-trendy silver hair down to my freakishly long toes. The only thing I could add to make the description more accurate would be the tears raining down and puddling on the floor in front of my church seat because I can only 'hold it together' for so long. Then, waterworks.

And here's the craziest thing about it. I'll bet I can blurt out ten verses right now about trusting God. Giving Him my worries. Finding His peace. No joke! Here are a few for starters...

"Casting all your cares on Him, because He cares about you" (1 PETER 5:7 HCSB).

"Don't worry about anything, but in everything, through prayer and petition with thanksgiving, present your requests to God. And the peace of God, which surpasses all understanding, will guard your hearts and minds in Christ Jesus" (PHILIPPIANS 4:6-7 CSB).

"Peace I leave with you; my peace I give you. I do not give to you as the world gives. Do not let your hearts be troubled…" (JOHN 14:27 NIV).

You get the idea. In fact, you probably recited bits and pieces of those right along with me. So, if we know what the Bible says about trusting God, and if we believe God can be trusted, how do we shift from knowing God to walking in steadfast trust in Him?

As I began researching the idea of living with unwavering trust in a God who was already very present in our lives, I hit a snag. Book after book pointed me to the solution for a life of worry: just trust God. For a life of frustration: trust God. Living with crippling doubt: trust God. They even drew verses from the Bible to support the idea, but something was missing. I already knew I needed to build up my trust game, but I didn't know *how* to do it. Because no matter what I tried, I still felt frazzled when daily demands were at an all-time high. And the really awful stuff? Forget it. Those things were my complete undoing, which translated into me trying to make it through each day, wishing the next would be better. As you take in these words that come from a vulnerable place in my heart, you may be asking yourself that question, too: *do I live like I trust God?* Or maybe you're wondering if you display that kind of faith-filled life to those around you. That's a hard question and one only you can answer. So let me offer a few thoughts to help you begin to work through it. If you would nod your head *yes* to any of these situations, you may be ready to up your trust game right along with me:

- When you pray about a big decision, do you then try to figure out all the possible outcomes?

- Do you sometimes feel personally responsible for your loved ones' choices?

- Do you intervene on your child's behalf when it's not a threatening situation?

- When an open door is in front of you, do you analyze it from every angle?

- Are you prone to changing your mind about something if it isn't working out the way you planned?

- Do you tend to jump in and help rather than let God work it out?

- Do you wait until there is no good solution before trusting God with the answer?

- Do you automatically imagine the worst-case scenario?

- Do you stay awake at night thinking about a problem you're facing after you've prayed about it?

- Do you complain about an issue to your spouse, co-workers, or friends, then feel guilty for complaining?

If you answered yes to any of these (with or without the accompanying nod), I have good news. No, scratch that. I have *amazing* news. The simple act of confirming where we are now invites our Heavenly Father to work in us like never before. For those of us who might say, "You know Kristine, these things don't apply to me and where I am in my life," amazing things await you as well. Because all we have to do is acknowledge our need for more of Him to experience that same invitation.

So now that we understand our starting place, let's begin our journey of learning from Rahab how to live with unwavering trust in an unfailing God.

Have We Met?

Before we venture back to around 1400 B.C., to one of the most significant moments in the history of God's people, let's get to know the woman of the hour. She may not have attracted much admiration back then, but she earned her rank as a faith hero for future believers. In fact, she's honored in the "examples of faith" roll call in the book of Hebrews.[1]

The local high school of my small town boasts a long hallway filled with "wall-of-fame" photos of graduates who've done great things. Considering the size of our town, it's quite impressive. Rahab's life may not have led her to be pictured on any wall-of-fame where she grew up, but I'd definitely include her in mine. She has earned my respect while also earning a forever place in my heart. Though thousands of years separate us from Rahab, we can refer to her as a soul-sister. Her life will be the catalyst that launches us into a deeper trust in our Creator. But I'm getting ahead of myself. Let's meet this feisty lady.

I make it a point to shine a light on someone's best qualities. It's a habit I've grown to love since God let the words of Ephesians 4:29 pierce my spirit. "Let everything you say be good and helpful, so that your words will be an encouragement to those who hear them" (NLT). It hasn't always been that way. Before meeting Jesus, I would've been the first in the group to judge another girl based on the way she dressed, where she lived, or her life choices. I would've made my opinions known, no holding back. But thanks to grace, God has worked to chisel away the rough and *really rough* edges, changing me into a better version of myself one chip at a time. So rather than focusing on what we may or may not already know about her past, let's meet Rahab with an untarnished perspective.

Also Known As

Travelers spotted her from every direction, whether inside or outside the city gates. Who could miss such a striking woman? "One of the most beautiful I've ever seen," men no doubt declared with an elbow nudge.[2] Tempted to avoid eye contact, women risked a bite by the jealousy bug each time her husband glanced Rahab's way. Her deep brown hair tied back to keep from getting in the way while pressing flax into a tub of water or spinning dried flax into linen. Still, wisps fell over her shoulders, a lovely sight rarely seen on married women because head coverings stifled any free-flowing locks.

Women also knew her home situated in the outer wall of town meant the whispers they heard held truth. In a city running amuck with sin, the sketchiest in society lived there. Yet Rahab didn't cower. She knew how to handle even the rowdiest men.

Single and self-employed, only an industrious woman would find ways to provide for herself and her family. Being able to eat, have a place to live, and protect yourself without a husband around? Practically unheard of for that time. Just ask Naomi and Ruth. After losing their husbands, Naomi needed Ruth to resort to placing herself among the poor, gleaning leftover grain so they'd have the means to live.[3] Single women were short on choices—an important detail to keep in mind when we're tempted to question what they did to survive.

Bundles of flax drying on her home's hot, flat roof ensured extra income. It would've been hard enough to fend for herself, but Rahab took responsibility for her relatives, too. A responsibility she welcomed with love and commitment.

Day after day this stunning, hardworking, devoted woman lived defined by choices likely made for her long before she could choose for herself. Rahab was a prostitute. Some scholars believe she also ran her home as an inn for travelers coming and going through the busy city entrance, but her role as a prostitute seems undisputed. We don't know what happened in Rahab's life to lead her to that place. Was she widowed at a young age? Forced into giving herself away? We can't let our wandering minds go there, but I do wonder with all the sincerity in my heart. Did other women talk to her, besides her own mother and sisters? Or did she hear the word *outcast* spoken by high-society types strolling past? *Maybe it was just the wind.*

So often we fall into the trap of condemning one another. Judging when we don't know the whole story. But not us, my friends. Not today. We won't gasp, shake our heads, or cast condescending looks. We will simply acknowledge the facts for the sake of God's daughters everywhere.

We are "made in God's image" and defined by Him alone. We have no idea what difficulties from Rahab's past shaped her current situation, but we will soon discover how her decisions took a drastic turn in the right direction.

Weaving a New Cord

In Rahab's day, women would often weave fine linen to create cord. Some were made of flax, just like the flax drying on Rahab's roof.[4] Women used the cord for various household chores like measuring, tying up a tunic, or even yoking animals.[5] In the same way, God weaves us together with other women to create one beautiful story, which we will see unfold through the pages of this book. "A cord of three strands is not quickly broken" (ECCLESIASTES 4:12B NIV).

The details of Rahab's life will provide the foundation for our trust journey. As we embark on the adventure with her—taking a glimpse of other sisters' stories along the way—I will show you how her actions impacted my own. How God transformed my trust-walk with Him through the power of this woman's testimony. And with each step in God's plan, we will all discover a foundation principle we can apply to our own journey of trust. Principles that will help us choose freedom over frustration, belief over doubt, decisiveness over worry, and faith instead of stress.

In the introduction, I shared a painful yet defining event in my life. There is more to the story, and I plan to tell you about many God-moments. Before I do, allow me to reveal our first foundation principle. Our starting point.

You see, it took a new kind of strength for me to resist looking at the doctor's diagnosis concealed in the envelope. An unfamiliar strength. Every out-of-control thought encouraged me to rip open the envelope and put my hope in the words I would find there. But I couldn't learn to really trust God unless I began with a humble confession. Our first foundation principle is this:

Moving to a new level of trust begins with knowing real change is possible and acknowledging we need help getting there.

Did I ever go back to that unopened envelope? Did I waver, leaving my new resolve and returning to a place of doubt? Those answers and much more await us in the coming chapters, and even though I'm giddy about getting there, I also feel good about *here*. Rather than letting bad news unravel us, we're ready to see real change happen. You, me, and Rahab. So, what are we waiting for? Let's take the all-important first step together with a Scripture-based prayer. Let's grab our strands and get ready to weave a new cord of hope. Our journey begins with this verse:

"I pray that God, the source of hope, will fill you completely with joy and peace because you trust in him. Then you will overflow with confident hope through the power of the Holy Spirit" (ROMANS 15:13 NLT).

Untying Old Habits

At the end of each chapter, we will pray a prayer to help us untie the knots of old habits and make room for God's truth. Then we will take a solid step forward as we "live it out." Let's begin with this prayer.

Dear Heavenly Father,

Thank you for this faith-filled journey, and thank you for giving us friends to travel with as we anticipate the adventure ahead. We know you can be trusted, Lord. But for whatever reason, we've struggled to believe in you like we know is possible. We also know we need to be willing to change in order to experience the victorious living you promise us when we fully trust you with our decisions, relationships, and hard things.

Your Word says in Romans 15:13 that you will fill us with joy and peace because we trust in you. Teach us the meaning of those words through Rahab's story, so we can enjoy abundant living with you. Thank you in advance for touching our hearts through the pages of this book and for the testimonies of your goodness that will come. In Jesus' name, Amen.

Living It Out: Weaving My Cord

In Rahab's day, women often wove fine linen to create cord. In the same way, God weaves us together with other women to create one beautiful story. In what areas of your life do you need the support of other women through prayer or encouragement?

In what areas of your life have you felt completely unraveled? Bring those before the Lord today, then watch how He begins restoring your hope. Hope that will hold firm for whatever lies ahead.

CHAPTER 2

Shutting the Gate on Worry

WHEN MY PROBLEM KEEPS ME UP AT NIGHT.

"But I am trusting you, O Lord, saying, 'You are my God.'"

PSALM 31:14 NLT

Acacia Grove brimmed with beauty and purpose. Nestled in the foothills just seven miles east of the Jordan River, it offered temporary dwelling for God's people. The Israelites had been traveling for a long time. Their leader Joshua had been here before. Forty years ago, in fact. I wonder if he knew then, when Moses sent him and eleven others to scope out the land ahead of them, that he would one day lead the charge to claim their inheritance.

Maybe Joshua remembered how ten of the chosen men came back to Moses with an unfavorable report. He and Caleb were the only two who believed the Israelites could come through with a victory. He knew then how the bad news brought to Moses caused doubt to permeate the hearts of the people. Doubt soon turned to fear, and their hopes of crossing the Jordan River into the Promised Land would be postponed for many years. Now, Joshua had been appointed Moses' successor and the new leader of God's people, giving him the responsibility of guiding them to their promised home. Their time had come.

"Then Joshua secretly sent out two spies from the Israelite camp at Acacia Grove. He instructed them, 'Scout out the land on the other side of the Jordan River, especially around Jericho'" (JOSHUA 2:1A NLT).

On the other side of the river towered two fortified walls surrounding a city called Jericho. What awaited them behind those walls? No one knew. In order to form a strategic plan of takeover, Joshua needed intel. He sent two spies to gather critical information about the city's infrastructure. How interesting that Joshua chose to send only two men when Moses had sent twelve on the same mission so many years ago! Yet from all twelve of Moses' spies, only two brought good news. Only two came back encouraged. Only two looked at the cup as half full instead of half empty. Did Joshua learn from that decision and adjust his plan based on the possibility of discouragement? Maybe he discovered sometimes it's better to get the opinions of two instead of twelve. We don't know for sure. But we do know these two spies understood their mission and would follow through because this victory would be the most important one of all. The Expositor's Bible Commentary puts it this way: their "espionage mission was focused on Jericho, a formidable fortress guarding the pass leading westward. Jericho was particularly important as the scene of Israel's first military engagement in the Promised Land."[6]

Their very first battle.

"So the two men set out and came to the house of a prostitute named Rahab and stayed there *that night*" (JOSHUA 2:1B NLT EMPHASIS MINE).

We mentioned Rahab's profession in chapter one, but as her story begins, we should consider the possibility that by this point in her life, Rahab may have repented.[7] Either way, her profession isn't the subject of our focus here. How she handled her current circumstances says more about her character than past mistakes.

Rahab's home created the perfect cover for the two spies sent to investigate Jericho. First, its proximity to the entrance would provide a convenient exit, should the need arise for a quick escape. Not to mention the ability to see who all comes and goes throughout the day and night. Second, its position in the city wall gave the best view of the happenings within the gates. And of course, staying at the local prostitute's place would keep the town folks from knowing the spies' true intentions. It wouldn't seem at all unusual for travelers to be seen at Rahab's. These spies knew what they were doing when they chose to stay with her. They didn't wait or look at other options. They came to her house and "stayed there that night."

Nosey Neighbors

"But someone told the king of Jericho, 'Some Israelites have come here tonight to spy out the land.' So the king of Jericho sent orders to Rahab: 'Bring out the men who have come into your house, for they have come here to spy out the whole land'" (JOSHUA 2:2-3 NLT).

Before they'd even been there long enough to ask for a drink of water, word of the strangers' visit reached the king. It doesn't take long for a good rumor to start, and this one had the townspeople stirring. The very day—or the very *moment*—the spies arrived, whispers began. Surely this came as no surprise to Rahab, but it also left her without time to think about what to do. She had to act immediately.

"Rahab had hidden the two men, but she replied, 'Yes, the men were here earlier, but I didn't know where they were from'" (JOSHUA 2:4 NLT).

People can be so helpful sometimes. Other times, not so much. Still, I like to think Rahab's nosy neighbors had the best intentions. "Poor Rahab probably doesn't know the real reason these men are here," they likely gossiped as she shrugged off their questions. But the fact that she had already hidden them tells a different tale. She *did* know who they were and why they'd come. That's right; Rahab listened. She paid attention. Travelers from all over came through the gates of Jericho, telling stories about these people called the Israelites and the amazing things their God had done. Stories like the miraculous rescue from slavery, the Red Sea splitting in two, and sweet bread flakes falling from heaven. "...They know, Lord, that you have appeared to your people face to face and that your pillar of cloud hovers over them. They know that you go before them in the pillar of cloud by day and the pillar of fire by night" (NUMBERS 14:14B NLT).

It appears our Rahab had been gathering her own type of intel, and this girl knew how to use it.

Rahab didn't wait before hiding the men in a safe place. She didn't weigh out her options. She didn't pause to see how things would play out then run around in a tizzy before responding to the king's request. Oh no, not this clever lady. She acted in instant obedience. The moment they arrived, Rahab sprang into action. But as you well know, life-changing decisions are never easy. Rahab's next move would show a new kind of boldness. Courage that would put her very life in danger. Let's brace ourselves as we hear what she explained to the king's messengers.

"'They left the town at dusk, as the gates were about to close. I don't know where they went. If you hurry, you can probably catch up with them.' (Actually, she had taken them up to the roof and hidden them beneath bundles of flax she had laid out)" (JOSHUA 2:5-6 NLT).

Rahab lied.

This wasn't just any old run-of-the-mill lie, either. Not the type you can brush off as insignificant or cover up with excuses like, "I just didn't want to hurt their feelings." This lie held the potential for deadly consequences. She lied to the king! I'm sure most of us would advise a friend against hiding wanted criminals in her home and lying to the king about it. I for one would much rather play it safe than put myself in that situation. Of course, we can't condone lying, but we can empathize with her predicament. Even though she knew the repercussions for her dishonesty, she did what she had to do.

It didn't make sense. An unmarried woman? Responsible for her well-being and her family's, harboring spies? The choices she made went against common sense, the laws of the day, and playing it safe. So to see the big picture, we need to let go of the fact that she broke the rules and remember that God uses imperfect people to complete His perfect will. Let's allow the Holy Spirit to bring out the truths we need to know. In that decision to help God's people, Rahab demonstrated unwavering trust in His plan.

Calming the Decision-Making Chaos

Decisions and I have a shaky relationship. You see, I'm an overthinker. When a door of opportunity opens, I struggle with what to do. I overanalyze options and possible outcomes. I let it consume my thoughts until a decision is made. Unfortunately, that means loads of sleepless nights and frustrated mornings. I lay in bed praying about it, then wrestle with it until I finally fall asleep. I long to walk in the instant obedience Rahab demonstrated but end up back in the same pattern.

Rahab's actions offer hope for us overthinkers. She decided the minute the problem knocked at her door. But how did she know what to do? Wasn't she frantic, surprised, confused? Just the thought of having to make a decision that important in such a short time makes my face flush and my hands sweat. I would've gone into full-blown panic mode for sure, but not Rahab. She knew the secret to trusting God with her decisions.

"Cast your cares on the Lord and He will sustain you; He will never let the righteous be shaken" (PSALM 55:22 NIV).

Remember this from Psalm 55? Yep, it's one of *those* verses. The ones we talked about in chapter one. We know them by heart and can quote them in tough times. (Well, sort of.) We also know how hard this casting business can be. We want to toss it up, let God catch it, and go on with life. Instead, we cast over and over, never pausing in the peace and rest God gives. So how can we truly let this verse transform the way we make decisions and embrace peace?

Just Keep Casting

My stepdaughter loves to fish. As a little girl, she displayed incredible patience while waiting for a bite on her line. One cast into the murky pond, and she was good for a while. My son, on the other hand, didn't take to fishing like his sister or dad. His favorite activities required more movement than you'd find on a fishing trip. He'd prefer climbing a tree over the stillness of a floating bobber in the water. Still, we brought him along and tried to teach him the joys of fishing. We'd watch him cast and reel the line back to check for bait. Cast, and reel the line back to check for bait, even though his dad told him to leave the bait in the water. On and on, he just kept casting.

I can be like that sometimes when problems and decisions consume me. I cast my care on God, then reel it back in to see how things are going. I repeat the process, never leaving it with God long enough to let Him work. Thankfully our loving God doesn't chastise us for this compulsion to check on things. Some of us are equipped with the patience to wait on God, while others need more practice. It takes time for us to learn the benefit of leaving the line in the water and letting the fish do their thing. Just like my son learning to have a little faith in the fish to take the bait, we can learn to release control to God and rely on His guidance. Until then, we just need to keep casting every day. To keep practicing until we get into the habit of leaving our problems with God.

When reeling the line back in to check on God's progress becomes a pattern, the words of Psalm 46:10 reaffirm God's gift of peace, "Be still, and know that I am God! I will be honored by every nation. I will be honored throughout the world" (NLT). With this verse in mind, let's take a look at our second foundation principle.

Agonizing over a decision results in taking control away from the Holy Spirit and giving it back to ourselves.

By daily releasing control to God, we trust His peace to calm the decision-making chaos.

Moving to a new level of trust is not a one-time big decision but a continued daily commitment to release control and allow the Holy Spirit to guide us. Rahab knew this. Remember the intel she'd been gathering for years? Storing God's promises in her heart gave her the confidence to be moved by the Holy Spirit, even during great danger. We will walk in that same level of confidence as we cast those cares, even if, at first, we have to keep casting again and again.

Activating the Plan

The king's men had every reason to believe Rahab. They didn't argue before they took off after the spies. Once beyond the city's outer wall for the night, the gates closed behind them. Rahab had activated the plan, no turning back.

"So the king's men went looking for the spies along the road leading to the shallow crossings of the Jordan River. And as soon as the king's men had left, the gate of Jericho was shut" (JOSHUA 2:7 NLT).

Rahab's decisiveness in that moment inspires me, and I pray you sense it too. I've never excelled at decision-making. Not one of my greatest strengths. I think about what I would've done in her situation and cringe. I can totally picture myself telling the soldiers, "They went thataway!" Then watching them head out the gate without giving it a second thought. But just as soon as the gate closed—as soon as *finality* set in—I'd question what I'd done. I'd fear my lies would be found out and worry the men would return to arrest me. I wouldn't be able to sleep all night, listening for the creaking of an opening gate or footsteps approaching. I would've let second-guessing my decision unravel my peace.

When we follow our foundation principle and daily release control to God, we may not always feel peaceful. There may be times when we feel overwhelmed with the weight of the decisions we need to make. By following that principle each morning, we ensure His peace is with us even when we don't feel it.

Finality is scary. Making healthcare decisions for yourself or your aging parent. Administering a dose of tough love to your rebellious teen. Accepting or turning down a job offer that requires a big move. Whatever choices we face, the hardest part of making a big decision is watching the gate shut and realizing there's no turning back. Unless we know for certain we made a mistake, we must resist trying to fix things. Instead, we can practice trusting God with what follows and watching His sovereignty at work.

Soul-sister, you may be thinking back on a decision you avoided or one hovering over you right now. Let me encourage you with this. Rahab's action came as she trusted the Holy Spirit to guide her. The answer won't always be "act." It may be "wait." Sometimes the Holy Spirit will prompt us to make a decision right away like Rahab did in the passage above. Other times, waiting will be involved, giving us time to take a breath, pray, and seek God's direction. We will look more at what to do while we wait in chapter eight. For now, let's loosen that knot of control as we let God calm our hearts.

The Power of Shutting the Gate

I sat in the oncologist's office with my trusty 3-ring binder resting on my lap. I believe in being prepared, staying organized, and having a place to take notes. I listened to each muffled voice outside the door, wondering if the next one would signal the doctor's entrance.

With back-to-back exams and two biopsies in the past week, all we knew was this: a cancerous mass had been found. That's it. I'd prayed our upcoming conversation with the doctor wouldn't shake me.

The doctor shook my hand, then my husband's. He and two other specialists I would see in the coming days had been discussing my case. He looked at reports, asked about my symptoms and family history, and drew diagrams.

He informed us that ninety-five percent of this type of cancer fit the same classification. My case, however, did not. I fit somewhere in the rare five percent, which caused difficulty in determining the best treatment path.

Just great.

My doctors scoured medical journals on my behalf, searching for cases similar to mine. Unfortunately, because of the rarity, information was scarce. (No intel.) So just like Rahab, here I was facing life or death decisions, with no sure-fire solution in sight. I had to make the best choice according to the One True Source. I could try to force it all to make sense according to human logic, or I could trust in God's ways instead of my own.

"But I am trusting you, O Lord, saying, 'You are my God!'" (PSALM 31:14 NLT).

When we have a life-changing decision to make, why do we struggle? And why do we let problems keep us up at night when we know peace and rest are possible? The truth is hard to admit, but we need to say it. Admitting the truth will help us move one step closer to the peace we seek. "For God is not a God of confusion but of peace" (1 CORINTHIANS 14:33A ESV).

The reason for our struggle with decision-making? We want to know when we make a decision that everything is going to be okay. We want assurance. Thankfully, we can be assured of this. God is faithful, and He can be trusted with our deepest hurts. That is the only assurance we need.

Let's revisit the foundation principle for this chapter one more time. *By daily releasing control to God, we trust His peace to calm the decision-making chaos.* I had to apply the truth of foundation principle #2 the day I listened to everything the doctor shared about my situation. I had to commit to daily casting my cares on the Lord and resting in knowing He was in control. That day

I would make a plan and close the gate on the most important decisions of my life. No turning back.

Untying Old Habits

Here is a prayer to help you sense His peace and know that He is with you as your Helper, even when you don't feel or hear Him:

Dear Heavenly Father,

It's easy to get caught up in the craziness of daily life and forget about your loving presence. You are here with me, but worry draws my attention away from the Holy Spirit, who offers peace and calm in the midst of the chaos. Lord, in those times when decisions overwhelm me, help me stay aware of your presence. I know you will never leave me nor forsake me (DEUTERONOMY 31:6 NIV).

I know I can stay connected with you by offering short, simple prayers anytime. Words like, "Lord, I need you" or "I give you praise" will redirect my thoughts toward you and help me be aware of your leading. Lord, guide me along your path. When I have you, I don't need anything else. Thank you for the gift of your calming presence in my life. In Jesus' name, Amen.[8]

"Be strong and courageous. Do not be afraid or terrified because of them, for the Lord your God goes with you; he will never leave you nor forsake you" (DEUTERONOMY 31:6 NIV).

Living It Out: Shutting Your Gate

When we left the doctor's office that day, my husband and I prayed for God's peace and asked Him to intervene. This was the most troubling thing we'd ever faced, and we needed to seek Him above all else. So we made a decision to focus on God's Word *first*. We would seek his direction and trust the peace that surpasses human understanding before discussing our situation with others. And from that one simple decision, God's plan unfolded. We experienced much-needed peace as He activated each next step. And we needed that peace, because we were about to be led through dark places beyond what we could endure in our own strength.

Is there an area of life or a decision where you've left the gate open, just in case? Are the details of the situation causing chaos in your mind? Invite God to help you shut the gate and believe He will reveal your next steps. He is beckoning you to trust Him to take care of it.

CHAPTER 3

Building a Strong Shelter of Trust

I KNOW GOD IS REAL. SO WHY DOES MY MIND KEEP IMAGINING THE WORST?

"Let us hold on to the confession of our hope without wavering, since he who promised is faithful."

HEBREWS 10:23 CSB

"Had I just fallen asleep?" The semi-conscious thought formed. Peeking at the blurry clock, I noticed several hours had passed. I lay frozen in the dark, wondering how I'd slept so soundly after the doctor's appointment earlier that day. Since I still had a few hours before sunrise, I decided to stay in bed and pray. Who knows? Maybe a quiet conversation with God would help me drift back to unawareness. But I soon discovered God had other plans.

As I began whispering my prayers, my memory carried me back a couple of weeks. I walked toward my favorite seat at church like so many Sunday mornings, and when the worship music started, tears welled up again. I'd cried every single week for I don't know how long. *Just stop this. People are staring.* No matter how hard I tried, I couldn't stop. With the first strum on the guitar, tears formed and multiplied as they leaked out.

Leading up to this recent turn-of-events, my husband and I had been pushing through a difficult season at home, like wading in mud. And honestly, we had more questions than answers. Even though we'd prayed, sought the Lord, and tried everything, we didn't feel any closer to a peaceful end. Frustrations in our home rose to an all-time high. Instead of raising my hands in worship, I was ready to throw my hands up in defeat.

Each week rolled into the next. Pray. Survive. Go to church. Cry. Pray. Survive. Go to church. Cry. Until this particular Sunday, when our pastor saw my tears and rose from his usual seat on the platform. He came over to me and said something I will never forget.

"You know God's got this, right?" It was a question, not a statement. One which stopped my tears mid-stream. Because even though I nodded *yes,* I hid the truth.

No, I didn't know.

Pastor David's question revealed a big problem that, until now, I refused to acknowledge. And it didn't have to do with my parenting, my husband, or even our circumstances. In true God fashion, He showed me what I hadn't seen all along. When it comes to trusting God, there's a life-changing difference between *knowing* it and *living* it.

The Three Trust Levels

In conversations with women both in-person and through social media, I discovered we're not alone in our longing to trust God more. We all want to rest knowing God has everything handled and our best interest in mind. Yet even with this desire, we still allow our thoughts to drift toward the terrible things that can happen. We question whether we hear God in the midst of our uncertainty, and we live with endless worry. But God wants us to build our trust on Him and to accept the peace and rest He gives. Peace and rest. Sounds amazing, doesn't it? We read a lot about peace and rest. We know they exist and love the idea even though they seem elusive.

Chasing peace and rest can send us into a pattern of defeat. It seems counterproductive at best and downright exhausting, too. Stress and worry take over, leaving peace and rest always just out of reach. There is a way to replace worrisome thoughts and feelings of frustration, but we need to establish where we are *now* in our level of trust first. Then we can determine how to construct from here.

In the accompanying workbook, you'll find a few simple questions to help you determine which level of trust best describes you at this time. Keep in mind that there are no right or wrong answers. The purpose of the quiz is to help us strengthen our ability to trust God, not to point out our faults or feel like our levels don't match up with the next girl's. As Paul said in Romans 8:1, "There is therefore now no condemnation to them which are in Christ Jesus, who walk not after the flesh, but after the Spirit" (KJV). I designed the quiz to guide us as we seek to walk "after the Spirit" toward a deeper relationship with our Creator.

The second thing to remember is this. The trust levels are like stone blocks in a wall, each one important. With each block, our shelter becomes stronger, more fortified. Our shelter will not stay the same forever. Our goal, wherever we are now, is to keep building layer upon layer.

In the pages ahead, we will explore three foundational levels for trusting God. Although each of us varies according to our unique experiences, we will all identify most with one of these levels. To describe them, let's return to Rahab, where we left her in the last chapter. The spies hid under drying flax on her roof, and Rahab lied to the king's men. At her suggestion, the king's men left Jericho in search of the spies, and the gate closed for the night. With the soldiers away, Rahab had a chance to talk to the two Israelites. Her conversation reveals the three trust levels and how they work together to form a strong dwelling place.

"Before the spies went to sleep that night, Rahab went up on the roof to talk with them. '*I know* the Lord has given you this land,' she told them. 'We are all afraid of you. Everyone in the land is living in terror. For we have heard how the Lord made a dry path for you through the Red Sea when you left Egypt. And *we know* what you did to Sihon and Og, the two Amorite kings east of the Jordan River, whose people you completely destroyed'" (JOSHUA 2:8-10 NLT EMPHASIS MINE).

The Knowledge (Believing) Level

Rahab had every reason to flat kick those spies right out of her house. Don't think for one minute she was too timid or afraid to do such a thing. We know better than that. Remember, Rahab had intel she'd gathered for years. Now for the first time, she came face-to-face with actual warriors from the Lord's army. Right here, on her very own roof! Asking them to leave was the last thing on her mind. She had waited for this chance and intended to make the most of it. She didn't ask them to tell her a glorious story of God's miracles or wonder about their next steps. She already knew about their God.

"I know the Lord has given you this land…" — Rahab

Many of us identify with the Knowledge Level of trust. We know God is real. We believe He exists and even agree He is trustworthy. This is a necessary first layer for a life of faith. There are some who believe in God and choose to follow Him. There are also those who believe there is a God but haven't invited Him into their lives. Either way, a knowledge of God is present. Rahab was rockin' the Knowledge Level. She had heard all the stories and shared them with her family. She chose to believe.

Let's allow our thoughts to drift back to the moment we first came to know about God. Did a parent tell you? Did you learn about Him in Sunday School or Vacation Bible School? Or maybe a dear friend shared with you how a loving Father changed her life and invited you to know Him too. However you were introduced, chances are you wanted to know more. More about this God who breathed everything into being in six days and sent His only son to save us from our sins. Your Knowledge Level began construction as your heart opened to the possibility of knowing Jesus.

In her book *Trust without Borders*, writer Arabah Joy says, "You can't trust a God you don't really know, in actuality. And you can't leave knowing God to happenstance."[9] Knowing there is a God who loves us changes our perspective. It brings structure to an otherwise shaky future. Because when we know He is real and that He wants a relationship with us, our world opens to new possibilities beyond what we can imagine. From the *knowing*, we begin the *trusting*.

The Verbal (Affirming) Level

"No wonder our hearts have melted in fear! No one has the courage to fight after hearing such things. For the Lord your God is the supreme God of the heavens above and the earth below" (JOSHUA 2:11 NLT). — Rahab

Rahab declared her belief with words, and without wavering.

If I asked you today who God is, what would you say? Let's think about that question for a moment. Maybe you'd say God is the Creator of the heavens and the earth or that He is your Father. Maybe you'd say He is all-knowing or that He holds us in the palm of His hand. You might say He is the One who provides the way to eternal life or even that God is love. If anything similar to these resonates with you, you can identify with Rahab's need to proclaim to the spies what she knew about who God is. When we say something is true, we profess our hope. By *saying it*, we proclaim the trusting.

The Verbal Level adds a new layer of solidity to our trust shelter. It describes those of us who say we trust God, pray daily, and read or memorize Scripture now and then. Because of our belief in God, we devote time to Him and learn from His Word. We understand the concept that God is in control of the outcome, not us. After all, the idea of trusting God echoes through many familiar verses, like this one. "Trust in the Lord always, for the Lord God is the eternal Rock" (ISAIAH 26:4 NLT).

I'd say I'm pretty proficient at this level. Enjoying my daily Bible reading plan with a cup of coffee ranks up there at the top of my *favorite things to do* list. Yes, the Verbal Level is where I've spent quite some time. In fact, many of us find our comfy place right smack in the middle of the Verbal Level.

The Verbal Level is a good place. I like it there. I even put down my building tools and kick back for a bit at this level. But sometimes the good can draw us into staying put by providing comfort and solace from the uncertainty of the world. It offers flannel pajama pants, a worn-out recliner, an episode or two of a favorite show, and maybe even a she-shed. Just enough to distract us from our cares for a while. If I choose to linger too long, I risk the long-term peace and rest God promises to those who trust in Him.

Rahab declared God as the "supreme God." She set herself firmly in the Verbal Level, but she didn't stop there. She took that all-important next step. Because as we well know, there's more to a life of trust than words. Rahab followed her saying with doing, and not just any doing. This was a *bold, in-your-face, trust-like-*

never-before kind of doing. The kind that inspired me to get up off that recliner once and for all, grab the cement, and start building the next level.

The Active (Doing) Level

"Now swear to me by the Lord that you will be kind to me and my family since I have helped you. Give me some guarantee that when Jericho is conquered, you will let me live, along with my father and mother, my brothers and sisters, and all their families" (JOSHUA 2:12-13 NLT). — Rahab

But Rahab, what about the kings' men? Aren't you worried they might return and take you prisoner? What will the king do to your family if he finds out you made a deal with the enemy?

Anyone else talk to the person on your page and warn them of impending doom? Then you understand how easy it is to trade our strong wall of trust for the worst-case scenario trap. I knew we were soul-sisters. I'm almost speechless at Rahab's calm demeanor. Because just like a hard season, Rahab's deal leaves us with way more questions than answers. It's what we do with those questions that determines whether we're ready to move to the Active Level of trust.

In the Active Level, we've shifted from knowing God or saying we trust Him to actively living out that trust in our everyday lives. This is where Rahab resided. She presented an offer with these words: "...give me some guarantee…" Rahab took action by requiring the spies to take action. If she truly believed they could save her, then she had to put complete control in their hands. The NIV puts it this way, "swear to me by the Lord that you will…"

She moved from declaring him as God to trusting *in Him* as God.

In her book *Little Women Big God*, Debbie W. Wilson wrote, "Sometimes, those of us who have been blessed with Bible knowledge are tempted to assess our faith by how much we know rather than by what we do with what we know. Rahab had little personal knowledge of the one true living God, but at the risk of her own life, she put every bit of what she knew into practice."[10] And from her belief, declaration, and decision, we can learn to live in the Active Level as well.

Worst-Case Scenario Game

I recently watched an episode of a popular show where the mom and dad faced the daily challenges of raising three daughters. As the girls grew and became more able to understand the struggles of life, the parents taught them a game they liked to call "Worst-Case Scenario." The purpose of the game, according to the parents, was to face their own fears by pointing out the worst thing that could happen in a given situation. They explained to their daughters how looking at the worst outcome would help them overcome their fears.

I'm not sure I agree with the philosophy of the game these fictional parents created. I do agree, living under the cloud of *all the bad things* can be devastating. As a young mom, I fought the enemy of my own imagination. I made daily decisions based on fear of the worst-case scenario. If my son wanted to have a sleepover at a friend's house, I conjured up all the potential horrible things that could happen. If he wanted to try out a new skateboard ramp, I stood close enough to catch him, just in case. Most of the time, the thing I imagined never really happened.

After years of worrying about potential outcomes and several wrinkles to prove it, I found the key to the peace and rest I'd been missing. And it was right there in Rahab's story. I learned to think of each problem according to God's Truth and use my imagination for good.

"Now to him who is able to do immeasurably more than all we ask or imagine, according to his power that is at work within us" (EPHESIANS 3:20 NIV).

Imagination is a powerful thing. It can create beauty and instill hope, or it can create worry and instill fear. Either way, we all have an imagination and the choice of how we will use it. Our imaginations can become an unsafe shelter, leaving us unaware of where we are in our trust relationship with God. Instead of letting our imagination lure us into all the terrible things, we can let it bring us as close to Jesus as possible.

Rahab solidified her trust by working on all three levels. With these cemented in place, there is no space left for the worst-case scenario. Our chapter Foundation Principle is this:

We build a strong shelter of trust in God when we move from knowing, to saying, to doing.

Adding Another Layer to My Shelter

When I lay in bed that quiet night thinking back to the words Pastor David spoke, I realized something. (Funny how quiet moments with God can do that. Help you realize things.) I had been stuck in the same place for so long I didn't even recognize it. I had gotten used to the constant stress and worry. I started each day more defeated than the day before until I lived in survival mode. I thought about this illness I now faced. It was my worst-case scenario.

I continued whispering my prayer, "Well God, I guess you have a reason for all this, so I accept it. There must be something you want to teach me, but I'm worn out. I just don't feel ready to go through another hard thing."

And in the same way that my tears stopped flowing with the pastor's words, "You know God's got this, right?" I sensed God's answer in the tranquility. I needed to learn how to actively trust the God I claimed to know. How to hold without wavering to the hope I professed. Like Rahab's request of the spies for a guarantee, I needed to act on the promise I heard and trust God with the outcome. This choice would soon prove paramount, just as it did for Rahab.

Untying Old Habits

The Scripture prayer below will help us build on the Chapter 3 foundation principle: *We build a strong shelter of trust in God when we move from knowing, to saying, to doing.*

Dear Heavenly Father,

Your Word says you are my "ever-present help" (PSALM 46:1). Yet even though I know those words are true, I haven't been living like I believe them. I know you are trustworthy, but I haven't actively trusted you in all things.

Forgive me, Lord, for staying in that comfortable place of knowing and saying I trust you while not taking that bold step toward really trusting. I've given in to stress and let my imagination conjure up all sorts of bad things instead of finding peace through Jesus. Help me move from knowing you as God to trusting in you as God. Help me trust like Rahab and build a strong, stable foundation where I can dwell in the assurance of your presence.

I am ready to move to a new level of trust in you, Lord. In Jesus' name, Amen.

"God is our refuge and strength, an ever-present help in trouble" (PSALM 46:1 NIV).

Living It Out: Building a Strong Shelter of Trust

Rahab gathered intel then expressed her belief in knowing who God is through her words and actions. If someone asked you today, "Who is God?" how would you answer that question? What is one memory you hold onto to remind you of God's faithfulness?

CHAPTER 4

Input Overload

THE IMPORTANCE OF CREATING QUIET
AMID ALL THE NOISE.

"Fearing people is a dangerous trap, but trusting the Lord means safety."

PROVERBS 29:25 NLT

Invaded. Humiliated. Exposed. Treatments hadn't even begun, and I already prayed for it all to end. Each exam drew me into the depths of unease. A team of compassionate doctors and nurses provided every ounce of support possible. They knew the trauma. They'd seen it many times before. I glimpsed mercy in their eyes, felt the gentle hand on my shoulder, and heard the words telling me, "You're doing great. We're almost finished. Just a few minutes more…"

Four tests in one week left me vulnerable and puny. Not a great combination when a PICC line scheduled for the following

Monday signaled an ensuing uphill climb. My mind still reeled over all the information we'd been given. Instinct told me to start calling everyone we knew and asking for advice. I'm a relational person. I love my people, and I wanted to talk to them. All of them. But I already felt overloaded with input, and we'd barely begun. Confusion built instead of security in the truth.

I just needed time to think.

Someone Told the King

In a city accustomed to staying alert to the latest updates, news of Rahab's two secret visitors spread faster than a plague. The massive walls warned Jericho's travelers they could expect to be watched. In the case of the spies, word reached the king in record time.

They didn't need the internet or social media to get the word out on the happenings of the day, especially when it came to newcomers. Although it's easy to imagine what the posts might've said when two possible spies were seen whispering with Rahab just outside her door. Judgments, accusations, and pointing fingers would surely spread from all the shares. New versions of the story would be spun quicker than readers could keep up. Would the townspeople question what or who to believe as the story changed form and took on a life of its own?

At any given moment, I can click my phone to life with one hand and instantly be transported to a million different versions, opinions, and statistics related to the same event. With a simple tap, I have access to every news app and social media site of my choosing. It's a dilemma we face each day. How do we spot the truth, with all the information out there for us to take in? We love being informed. In our innate desire to learn all we can, we look at stories from every angle. Search for every possible source. Soon our innocent need to learn more turns into an addiction. An information addiction. And that need for a fix can overpower our ability to trust what's true.

As important as it is for us to keep learning and growing in knowledge, this input overload also has its vices. Vices so cunning, we won't even know we're being victimized by it. Information can be a good thing. Researching procedures led me to make a few tough calls in the midst of my health crisis. Finding that delicate line between what we need to know and too much information brings us to an important question in our trust walk. With all the voices in the world today shouting for our attention, how do we focus our mental energy in the right place? How do we listen with discernment and find what's true?

We may not be able to spot every fake news site out there, but God will draw us toward the source of all truth when we ask. We begin by acknowledging that our Source is different from the world's.

Creating Quiet in Our Thoughts

"Fix your thoughts on what is true…" (PHILIPPIANS 4:8 NLT).

Near the end of his letter to the believers at Philippi, the apostle Paul sent his church a clear message about the importance of their thought life. He gave a list of virtues we can still turn to today, "…what is true, and honorable, and right, and pure, and lovely, and admirable. Think about things that are excellent and worthy of praise." (PHILIPPIANS 4:8B NLT). Notice Paul began with the one element God knew we'd need as our world became more connected: the truth. Here we are, able to gather information with our fingertips. We know more people. We stay in touch from miles away. We translate languages in a snap and within seconds know what's happening across oceans. With so much information available to us, how do we know what or who to listen to? How do we fix our thoughts on what's true?

Truth for anything we face in life can be found in Scripture. Jesus himself affirms this in His prayer to the Father as recorded in John 17:17, "Sanctify them by the truth; your word is truth" (NIV). Our fragile minds are inundated with things that can cloud the truth for our circumstances. Fixing our thoughts on God's truth sounds doable, but it takes daily effort on our part. My childhood friend Dr. Jennifer Mundine said it well in a social media post, so I asked her permission to share it with you here. Jennifer says, "Change, in many cases, comes from little, daily steps of doing something different. I've heard that thoughts control your actions. But it has been the opposite for me. Actions that go against my thoughts have now changed my thinking."[11]

Controlling our thought life takes effort and action. Taking steps to fix our thoughts on what is true first will keep us from fixating on what or who to believe.

People-pleasing Problems

One thing that can get in the way of focusing our thoughts is our need to please the people in our lives. Faith-filled women love deeply and care ferociously, but that desire to see our people fulfilled and living their best lives can sometimes distort our thought life.

I'm a recovering people-pleaser, and hurting feelings is one of my biggest issues. I've been known to make a decision or two based on another person's opinion or seeking their approval. Not wanting to hurt feelings sounds like a good trait to have. I love being known as a conscientious person. But the gut-honest truth is, when I say or do things hoping to keep someone happy, I'm letting their feelings dictate my actions.

I could sense this temptation taking over when flooded with more medical information than I expected. I wanted to tell every person I knew about my current struggle and ask for their input on a battle strategy. But when everything inside urged me to pick up the phone and start calling, one thing stopped me. A gentle whisper, telling me I needed to face this battle quietly, at least for the moment. I didn't know why, but I was determined to resist the urge to seek input and trust God's guidance.

The basis for our urge to please others reaches much deeper than being a conscientious person. It speaks to our misplaced responsibility for their happiness and well-being. In real life, it could look something like this:

- You love being the one your boss comes to first because he knows you will get the job done. Until you end up doing not only your job but everyone else's too. Pretty soon, burn-out ensues.

- You're the first one to raise your hand to coach the soccer team, run for PTA president, and organize the bake sale. Until you realize you're too tired to enjoy time with the kids. You miss quiet nights at home as a family.

- You feel like you aren't helping your pastor enough because a good Christian would volunteer more at church.

You're beating yourself up inside for not doing your part, so you add more to your schedule. Bitterness rears its ugly head when no one else offers to help. Soon you question whether you want to attend church at all.

- You lay awake at night asking yourself why that certain person didn't respond to your text and wonder if you should reach out more, give more, and be a better friend. Until you entertain thoughts of rejection.

Ready for a confession? I usually stick to a one-confession-per-chapter limit, but I'm making an exception this time because it's important for you to know this. Each of the above scenarios came straight from my life's playbook, my friend. So, if you saw yourself in any of these situations, I'm right there with you. People-pleasing can be a problem that snatches away our ability to trust God fully. It places our worth and acceptance in others instead of the God who cherishes us for who we are.

So, how does people-pleasing affect our trust level? The Expositor's Bible Commentary offers people-pleasing wisdom related to the verse I shared at the beginning of this chapter, Proverbs 29:25. "True security is the result of trusting God and not other humans. Fear of others becomes a snare when it gets to the point of letting others control your life—their opinions and attitudes put subtle pressure on you, even hindering you from speaking the truth or doing what is right. Release from such bondage comes when people put their faith in the Lord alone."[12]

Notice the definition of *fearing people* here refers not to being afraid, but letting others control your life. Ouch. Anyone else feel a little sting with that one? Letting opinions and attitudes impact our thoughts—even from those we love—will alter our ability to discern what's best for us. Our ability to hold onto what's true. All the more reason for us to work on overcoming our need to please others.

Assumption, Assumption, What's Your Function?

Last Saturday my husband and I went on what we like to call a "date day." He started by asking where I wanted to eat lunch. Cue the decision drama.

So many choices! This took information overload to a whole new level. I couldn't keep my mind on just one thing. To narrow it down, I thought about what he *might* want to eat. No sense in asking since I assumed he'd say, "I don't care. You pick." Of course.

I put my keen detective skills to work. I could figure this out. First, I knew he was trying to eat low-carb, so I assumed he wouldn't want to go to an Italian or Mexican restaurant. Second, he never chooses seafood because I'm allergic. (He's considerate like that.) Third, we'd just had home-cooked vegetables the day before, so scratch that off the list. Okay, crisis resolved! I picked a restaurant where we could get soup or a salad. I didn't even ask his opinion or attempt to discuss it. I made assumptions based on the evidence, getting myself worked into a frenzy in the process.

Have you ever been there? Trying to figure out the best route, factoring in every detail like a word problem in your child's math homework that's left you dazed and confused? I can recall several times I've fallen into this pattern, and usually it involved some type of assumption on my part.

- When I don't get invited to eat lunch with a group of friends, I assume they don't like me. So I withdraw from those relationships.

- I read a certain tone in a pointed email and assume the sender is angry with me, so I hit *send* on a curt response of my own.

- My husband stares at his phone while I'm telling him something important. I assume he isn't listening, so I give him the silent treatment.

Assumptions are based on the unknown instead of the truth. They serve a purpose in scientific hypotheses or solving a good whodunnit mystery, but not in our daily life. God's truth is the only 100% reliable cornerstone for our focus in the trials we face.

After her brief interaction with the king's men at her door,

Rahab tiptoed up to the roof and talked to the spies. She could've let that affect her discernment in the moment, but instead she focused on what she knew to be true. Rather than wondering or guessing, she told them the truth she believed about their God. Then, she moved forward with that truth firmly secured.

We can recognize any assumptions we've been chasing and remove them from the equation. When we learn not to assume anything, we increase our trust in what God can do. Letting go of assumptions helps with decluttering unnecessary thoughts while pointing us back to what God's Word says. This idea will help when assumptions build up in our minds: *When I'm tempted to chase a trail of assumptions, I will focus on what I know to be true.*

We want to listen to God alone. We come to Him with good intentions but shift toward what *we think* should happen. How we feel the situation should work out, leaving little room for God to work in ways outside of what we imagine.

Have you ever prayed and asked God for guidance, only to start sharing your own agenda with Him? God gave us an intellect and wants us to use it, but those brains of ours can backfire. We take over, which keeps His power tucked in a jar when, in truth, there aren't enough jars on the earth to contain it. Our job is to believe in that power and not confine it. To listen and let God work.

A Woman Who Knew How to Trust

"One day the widow of a member of the group of prophets came to Elisha and cried out, 'My husband who served you is dead, and you know how he feared the Lord. But now a creditor has come, threatening to take my two sons as slaves'" (2 Kings 4:1 NLT).

Desperate times, desperate measures. This unnamed woman's late husband was a prophet, so she knew where to go for help. Still, how could she be sure Elisha could do anything? Her situation seemed beyond desperate. If the creditor took her two boys, she couldn't continue living. If the grief didn't overtake her, starvation surely would. So she did the only thing she could and appealed to Elisha. She hoped with everything in her being that he'd help.

"Tell me, what do you have in the house?" (2 Kings 4:2b NLT). The prophet's response seemed unorthodox but spoke volumes about God's wondrous works. The widow didn't need to look any farther than her own kitchen to display obedience to God's plan. To say *yes* to His overflow of goodness in her life. She didn't question but set her mind on the task and sent her sons to carry it out.

Throughout Scripture and in our own lives, God uses what we have to bring about big miracles. But we must be willing to obey. The crazy thing about it is His ways are straightforward, yet we struggle to follow. We allow things like pleasing others or making assumptions distract us from God's basic truth. Thankfully our all-knowing God has abundant life in store for those who rely on His guidance and take a faith step as He directs. "The fact that she herself was to act in faith would enlarge her faith" (Expositor's Bible Commentary). It was true for the widow, and the same is true for you and me!

God asked the widow to take a faith step. But before she would see His provision poured out in her life, He made sure to protect her from any distractions lurking around. He directed her to go into the house and shut the door behind her.

"And Elisha said, 'Borrow as many empty jars as you can from your friends and neighbors. Then go into your house with your sons and shut the door behind you'" (2 KINGS 4:3-4A NLT).

Closing herself in her house shielded her from what other people might say or think. It protected her from unnecessary input. She trusted God's power over her own agenda. And just like when the gate shut in Jericho and sealed Rahab's decision to conspire with the spies, this widowed mom of two boys would soon see what happens when you obey God. She would do what the prophet told her to do without listening to all the other voices. She would focus on what was true.

"'Pour olive oil from your flask into the jars, setting each one aside when it is filled.' So she did as she was told. Her sons kept bringing jars to her, and she filled one after another. Soon every container was full to the brim! 'Bring me another jar,' she said to one of her sons. 'There aren't any more!' he told her. And then the olive oil stopped flowing" (2 Kings 4:4b-6 NLT).

I can relate to this righteous woman's need to shut the door. Just like the story I shared with you at the beginning of this chapter, God has shown me time and again the importance of putting my mental energy toward what is true rather than getting tied up in all the voices. All the opinions. All the information. By urging me to create some much-needed quiet at the start of my most difficult battle, God gave me a great gift. He gave me room to hear Him above all else.

Maybe you, too, can relate to why the prophet insisted the widow shut the door on some things in her life. Maybe like me, and Rahab, and so many other women, you've longed for God's guidance but gotten lost in the vast amount of noise you hear. You believe, but find it harder each day to focus on what is true. If you could only declutter your thoughts, you know you would hear God. Friend, could I give you a virtual high-five, fist-bump, and long-distance hug right now? Because we understand each other, flaws and all. And I am so glad we can discover together the victorious living that awaits when we identify the things in our thought-life that hinder us. Let's look back at the verse we began with in this chapter but in a different version. "The fear of human opinion disables; trusting in God protects you from that" (PROVERBS 29:25 MSG). Our next foundation principle is this:

> *When I trust God amid all the noise, confusion clears away, revealing His truth for my trial.*

In whatever area of your life you need to trust God right now, let's take a moment to let the confusion slip away while we invite His peace. Opinions, advice, and information can be a good thing, but we need to return our focus to our One True Source. He is always faithful, and His Word will never fail us. Create quiet right now. Focus only on God.

Untying Old Habits

Dear Heavenly Father,

When I think about the times I've struggled to trust you, I realize I get confused by all the information calling for my attention. It is hard to sift through it all and focus on you. But when

I keep your Word at the center of my heart and mind, I discover the power in your truth.

Psalm 40:4 says, "Blessed is the one who trusts in the Lord, who does not look to the proud, to those who turn aside to false gods" (NIV). Help me remember this when I lean toward people-pleasing, making assumptions, or wanting to figure things out on my own. You are the one true God. You are for me, and your way is always best. Help me to keep that affirmation deep in my spirit. I give my information addiction over to you today, Lord. I let it go. You are my One True Source. In Jesus' name, Amen.

Living It Out: Creating Quiet to Make Room for What's True

The last thing I needed was to add more information to my already overloaded thoughts. Once I created quiet time to focus on promises from God's Word, I felt more secure. Confusion began to clear away.

I called three people to ask them to pray—a family member and two close friends. God's reason for the discretion He asked of me earlier became clear as He affirmed His truth through these calls. All three people said the same *three things*, nearly word-for-word.

Three people, three things. God is so good! First, they expressed a sincere knowing that this would be a hard-fought battle. Second, they sensed a certainty I would come out of the battle victorious. And third, that God would use my testimony to encourage others going through similar circumstances. That's when I knew. God wanted me to fix my thoughts on what was true, so He could then verify that truth through the testimony of three trusted people.

Tightening my grip on the God-inspired words my loved ones shared would replace my confusion with trust in God's plan. Clearing away all the extra voices would keep my faith in the One who had everything under control.

In Rahab's town, word spread fast about the spies. News and information can send our minds spinning, causing confusion. In what ways can you focus your thoughts the next time you feel overloaded with input?

CHAPTER 5

The Power in the Promise

I PRAYED, SO WHY DO I KEEP OVERANALYZING
ALL THE POSSIBLE OUTCOMES?

*"Our Lord, you are true to your promises, and your word is like silver heated
seven times in a fiery furnace."*

PSALM 12:6 CEV

The stone steps chilled the balls of Rahab's calloused feet as she stole away to the rooftop. She'd prepared many meals up there, dried food and textiles, and attended to an array of other chores made easier under the lasting sunlight the shadeless roof gave. But this task could only be risked under the cover of darkness.

She needed enough light to illuminate the steps, but not enough to be visible by any neighbors sneaking around in the night. Her pottery DIY project would do the trick— a handcrafted vessel with a wick and a little oil. Cupping the makeshift lamp, Rahab took each step while preparing her heart for the next step in the plan.[13]

I wonder what thoughts whisked through her mind when she "went up on the roof to talk" with the spies hiding there. No doubt she'd considered her options. But I can't help but linger in those few moments just before. That crucial time on the stairs, between her sleeping family and a life-changing conversation with two strangers. Rahab cared about her family. Being a take-charge kind of girl, maybe she thought about how her choice would affect them. How much they would struggle if anything happened to her. With all the things she could've considered, only one question needed to be: *would Rahab protect her family in the moment, or trust God to protect their future?*

She approached. We know the conviction she showed. We saw it in Chapter 3, where we learned how this choice demonstrated her cross over to the Action Level of trust. Did the knowledge of God's sovereignty whisper hope to her heart? A psalm of King David that wouldn't be written for generations seems fitting to Rahab's need. "Trust in the Lord and do good. Then you will live safely in the land and prosper" (PSALM 37:3 NLT).

Looking back at the record of Rahab's words, we might be tempted to think her request for a guarantee from the Israelites was just that—a request. But it wasn't. It wasn't a question, a suggestion, or an idea to consider. It was a command. "*Give me some guarantee.*"

What boldness. What assurance! She spoke to them as her equals, not someone she needed to kneel before or put on a pretentious show. No time for that nonsense. They must make their move before losing any more time, so Rahab got right to the point. And the spies' next statement sealed the deal.

"'We offer our own lives as a guarantee for your safety,' the men agreed. 'If you don't betray us, we will keep our promise and be kind to you when the Lord gives us the land'" (JOSHUA 2:14 NLT).

Guaranteed.

I have a tendency to over-apologize. I will start sentences with, "I'm sorry, but…" and then say what I want to say. It's that fear of hurting feelings again. Gets me every time. Yet even though my intentions are to speak with grace and love, my overmodest opener can send the wrong message. It communicates that I'm uncertain about what I have to say. That I lack confidence. Grace and love are an essential part of how we build relationships as women of faith. They soften hearts and open doors, giving us opportunities to share Jesus with our people. The Bible is filled with wisdom regarding how we talk to one another, and grace and love top the list. "Let your speech always be gracious, seasoned with salt, so that you may know how you ought to answer each person" (COLOSSIANS 4:6 ESV).

Yet our longing to "season our speech with salt" sometimes turns to apprehension about how we come across to others. We develop a fear of what people think of us, and it overflows into what we say. The good news is we don't have to sacrifice grace for confidence in the truth.

Jesus came as the perfect balance of grace and truth. John 1:17 tells us, "For the law was given through Moses; grace and truth came through Jesus Christ" (NIV). Jesus showed us through how He lived that grace and truth work in harmony. Our personalities and life experiences will pull us more toward one or the other, but our Savior's example encourages us to keep moving toward a balance of both.

Remember Rahab's bold words, "give me some guarantee"? Her statement is an example of an imperative sentence, one of four sentence types. It begins with a verb instead of a subject and gives a command. *Do* your homework. *Wash* the dishes. *Run* for your life. An imperative sentence can create an essence of courage. Certainty. The situation called for urgency, no doubt. Rahab knew what she needed, and she communicated that without an abrasive tone. Rahab's words showed a confidence that could only come from knowing the source of her strength and the source of the Israelites' mission.

In the last chapter, we learned our Source is different from the world's. Now we understand, there is assurance in knowing our

Source. Author Abby McDonald put it this way:

> "So often, I base my security on the need for a guarantee. And since there are few guarantees in life, I'm left restless and floundering. But the fact is, I do have a guarantee. And so do you. I am guaranteed Christ's presence, and bright hope and future, no matter what. I'm promised that his peace will surround me as I choose to focus on his character rather than the things I don't yet know."[14]

Sometimes we forget God's promises. Those are our guarantees. Life without a promise to hold onto leads to uncertainty. That uncertainty will leave us powerless, unable to enjoy a confident, trust-filled life. But like Rahab, we can practice boldness by reframing our words. We can take our cue from her and learn to communicate with not only grace and love but confidence in what God can do.

Let's Make a Deal

"Then, since Rahab's house was built into the town wall, she let them down by a rope through the window" (JOSHUA 2:15 NLT).

Rahab's skill at crafting necessary things for her household proved handy. She didn't have to hunt long to find a length of rope for aiding the spies in their escape. Quick thinking on her part revealed this thought: Sending them through the front door now that the king knows they're here? Not a chance. There had to be a better way, and Rahab found it.

The king's men would be pursuing them in the direction of the Jordan, the quickest route to the Israelite's camp. So to lead them to the safest place possible, Rahab sent them in the opposite direction. To the hills west of Jericho where they'd find plenty of caves to hide in.[15]

"Escape to the hill country," she told them. "Hide there for three days from the men searching for you. Then, when they have returned, you can go on your way" (JOSHUA 2:16 NLT).

Did she anticipate the next words she heard? Did she understand the reason they extended her own red rope toward her, a gift that would serve a greater purpose than aiding their escape?

She'd trusted them to this point. No reason to stop now. Rahab listened, intent to remember every life-or-death detail.

"Before they left, the men told her, 'We will be bound by the oath we have taken only if you follow these instructions. When we come into the land, you must leave this scarlet rope hanging from the window through which you let us down" (JOSHUA 2:17-18A NLT).

There it was. All her hope for her future, all the uncertainty and the terrifying things she might face. All the time she'd spent caring for her family and preparing for the unknown. All of it, wrapped in the secure knot of a single red rope.

Putting Action to Our Faith

"Great faith, wherever it is found, is always rewarded, for it is pleasing to God" (Believer's Bible Commentary).[16]

We can be fickle with our faith. As we learned earlier in this book, building a solid foundation of trust begins when we replace saying with doing. In those shadowed moments right before we take action, we are vulnerable to the trap of trying to figure out the future. This need to have control of the outcome causes us to hesitate. To avoid the risk, because we can't see whether the risk is worth it.

The best way to avoid the trap of wavering faith is to follow Rahab's example of certainty in God's promise. That's where we find the power to take that faith step toward the unknown.

"Rahab ... was shown to be right with God by her actions when she hid those messengers and sent them safely away by a different road" (JAMES 2:25 NLT).

Like Rahab, adding action to our faith demonstrates our trust in God to provide. In her book *When You Need to Move a Mountain*, friend and faith writer Linda Evans Shepherd says this: "The more we focus on what we fear, the harder it becomes to trust God. Without trust, we cannot have faith. Without faith, our prayers are ineffective."[17] Focus, faith, and prayers. That's how we find the strength to trust in our Heavenly Father.

I'm not going to pretend for one minute trusting God with the unknown is easy. I'd like to tell you I've conquered my fears and learned to give it all to Him without giving it another thought. But that wouldn't be true, and if we've learned anything together, it's that honesty leads to growth. So let me be soul-bearing honest with you right here. Right now.

I struggle with putting action to my faith all the time. Sure, I make progress. Then I catch myself paralyzed by the possibility that things could go wrong and would rather just avoid the risk. But my pursuit to stay in the Active Level of trust keeps me focused on good things. It ensures I hold onto God's promises and let other things go. That means we have hope, my friends. Hope for change. Hope for growth. Hope for the future.

"And all your family members—your father, mother, brothers, and all your relatives—must be here inside the house. If they go out into the street and are killed, it will not be our fault. But if anyone lays a hand on people inside this house, we will accept the responsibility for their death. If you betray us, however, we are not bound by this oath in any way" (JOSHUA 2:18B-20 NLT).

My head would be swimming! "Wait a minute while I jot this down!" my frantic words would reveal the nerves I tried to hide. But not Rahab. I am blown away by her steadfast countenance at that moment. She did not falter as she sealed the deal with the spies.

"'I accept your terms,' she replied. And she sent them on their way..." (Joshua 2:21a NLT).

Details, Details

For God's covenant to be complete, Rahab couldn't deviate from the details. The spies instructed her to follow them with precision. Throughout the Bible, we find story after story where the Lord gave specific details for His people to follow, and Rahab was no exception.

Details are important to God. This reveals a valuable glimpse of God's character. He cares about every part of our lives, down to the smallest detail. "Indeed, the very hairs of your head are all numbered. Don't be afraid; you are worth more than many sparrows" (Luke 12:7 NIV).

No one knew this better than Mary, whose story can be found in John 11. Her brother Lazarus became sick. The outlook wasn't good, but she and her sister Martha sent for Jesus anyway (John 11:1-3). They prayed and put their faith in their Savior to come through with a miracle once again. His delay in returning only fed the agony the women felt watching their brother suffer. And even with all the prayers they could offer, Lazarus died.

To make matters worse, Jesus wasn't there.

"Lord, if only you had been here, my brother would not have died" (John 11:32b NLT). When Jesus showed up too late to heal

Lazarus, Mary let Him know about her disappointment. She assumed Jesus' delay affected the outcome, and it wasn't the one she wanted.

But Jesus had a different ending in mind. One based on the big picture rather than personal desires. One that would reach beyond their immediate family to the people watching, waiting, and mourning. Mary discovered something new about the definition of faith that day. A truth we can also find if we're willing to answer this burning question: *Do I trust enough to believe my struggle could be part of a bigger plan?*

It's one of the hardest concepts for us to grasp as women believers. The details of our lives are interconnected with others in such an intricate pattern that everything we face contributes to the greater good according to God's purpose. Jesus orchestrated his return to Bethany at a specific time because God planned to show up and perform a miracle unlike anything they'd seen.

Lazarus' body had been in the tomb so long that the smell would've been unbearable. Jesus left no question about the fact that Lazarus was dead. What better way to signify the unmatched power of God to resurrect our lives than to bring His friend back to life? "Jesus responded, 'Didn't I tell you that you would see God's glory if you believe?'" (JOHN 11:40 NLT).

Therein lies the answer to the burning dilemma. The one Mary faced, the one Rahab faced, and the one you and I will face over and over in our walk with the Lord. With all the possible outcomes, we must believe. God's way is best, so we fasten our hope to His faithfulness.

Cinching Her Trust

"After they had gone, she tied the scarlet cord to the window" (JOSHUA 2:21B CSB).

Rahab stared at the red rope gripped in her hand. She paused only long enough to be sure the spies had fled out of sight. Whether her stomach was tied in the very knot she needed to create, we do not know. Did she hear an inner voice whisper, "You know God's got this, right?" Did she consider all the glares from neighbors, wondering what in the world the *tiqvah*, or cord, was doing hanging in her window?

Upon first getting to this point in Rahab's story, I thought about whether Rahab ever reconsidered her action step. Whether she concocted the most fool-proof knot she could but then stopped short, allowing her analysis of the possible outcomes to steal her confidence. But a hidden truth in her story shows us she did not waver. How do we know this? What proof could we have to believe without a doubt in Rahab's steadfast trust in the God she claimed to know? Because the Hebrew word for "cord" has another meaning as well. The word "tiqvah," or cord, also means "what is hoped for" or "outcome."[18]

As she secured her tiqvah to the window, she also trusted the outcome to a God who would not fail. Our Foundation Principle is this:

Free yourself from the tangle of all the possible outcomes. Cinch your trust as tight as you can to God's guarantee.

Rahab's tying of the scarlet cord to the window signified her trust in the men to return for her and her family. No matter what happened, Rahab needed to hold onto that promise. In the same way, we cannot face life's biggest trials with confidence if we don't first agree with God in His steadfast promise for us.

Rahab's story teaches us we have an active part in the promise—to cinch it as tight as we can. To cease analyzing the possible outcomes and trust God with our future.

Untying Old Habits

Dear Heavenly Father,

Thank you for the promises found in your Word. I know those promises are your guarantees for my life and my loved ones, but I struggle with putting action to my faith. Forgive me for trying to figure out all the possible outcomes instead of trusting you in every situation. I want to learn how to stay in the Action Level of trust and move forward with confidence.

Lord, in the past I've lacked confidence in your Truth, many times letting grace and love be my excuse for not walking in assurance as a child of Almighty God. Help me develop confidence in my calling and allow the Holy Spirit to guide my steps. Psalm 119:105 says, "Your word is a lamp to my feet and a light to my path" (NKJV). May I discover steadfast trust as I let your Word direct me.

Thank you for teaching me how to trust you more. Thank you for the truth I am discovering through Rahab's story. Her red cord shows you have the best outcome for me, the best plan for my life. When faced with fear of the future, I will stay focused on your promises and accept your Truth as a guarantee. You are my Provider, my Refuge, and my Deliverer. In Jesus' name I pray, Amen.

Living It Out: Unwavering Faith

What tiqvah, or outcome, do you need to trust God with today? In what area of your life have you been reluctant to cinch your trust to God's guarantee? Freedom awaits as you release the need-to-know and rest in the truth that your struggle could be part of God's bigger plan. Write the chapter foundation principle on a sticky note and place it where you're sure to see it every day this week. Repeat it aloud as you experience renewed faith in God's powerful promises.

CHAPTER 6

Trading What-Ifs for Living As-If

How do I identify my promise?

"Understand, therefore, that the Lord your God is indeed God. He is the faithful God who keeps his covenant for a thousand generations and lavishes his unfailing love on those who love him and obey his commands."

DEUTERONOMY 7:9 NLT

Journal entry November 30th:

Today I'm finishing my first round of chemo. Physical exhaustion, fatigue, mouth and throat sores, constipation, pain. I. AM. TIRED. Blessings - texts from friends at just the right time. Morning devotions with Phil. (He reads it to me when my mouth is too sore to talk.) Listening to a worship song that reminds me God is with me, and He is FOR me. I cannot let physical pain and fatigue distract me. I must focus on God's presence, promises, and peace every single day. I'm seeing how easy it is to let my mind go down the wrong path. Praise helps me maintain trust. Reciting God's Word brings peace.

Picture Rahab's window with me, held firmly in place with the red cord. From a certain angle, the picture resembles a letter sealed shut, ensuring the safety of its contents until opened by the one who would receive it. Seals in Rahab's day and throughout the New Testament were often made of wax. A wax seal was even used on Jesus' tomb. The significance of a seal is a powerful thing. It represents a binding oath. A promise from the sender. "A seal, in biblical times as today, is used to guarantee security or indicate ownership."[19]

The moment Rahab tightened the cord to the outside of her window, she cinched her belief that God would take care of her and her family, come what may. She made the ultimate decision to hold fast to God's promise. Rahab traded analyzing outcomes for expectation in God's faithfulness. And in turn, God set His seal in place. He guaranteed her security. He would do what He said He would do. So how do we apply this same expectation to our own lives when we are at our weakest? How do we trust that seal to stay put?

Sealing the Deal

Two weeks after writing the journal entry above, I watched my husband hustle around the room through tears blurring my vision. He dressed in haste for Sunday service as we discussed what to do. I was having a rough morning, and he was expected at church an hour away.

Caring for me and caring for a congregation was a lot to handle. I strained to turn choppy breaths into deep, slow ones. The last thing we needed was for me to go into full-blown panic. I don't know what triggered this fear, but I just knew I couldn't be alone. Not today. I woke up with throat sores making it near impossible to swallow. With each attempt I felt like I would choke. Then what? Who would be here to help? We knew the unlikelihood of finding another pastor to fill in at the last minute. Guilt came alongside the fear I already battled. I had to be strong so he could leave. The church needed him, too.

But I was scared.

In a moment of revelation, my husband suggested calling a friend who lived close by. Just the thought of having her there with me ushered in easier breathing. Then, within mere seconds, the what-ifs began. Melissa directed the children's program at her church on Sunday mornings. What if she had already left home? What if she wasn't available to come and help? Thankfully Phil didn't let the what-ifs overshadow the hope he had in God to provide. He called.

Melissa answered and said she'd be right over.

I kept a journal of my journey through cancer treatments. I couldn't write every day; weakness wouldn't allow it. Still, I wanted to remember everything God did for me during that time. Here is a glimpse of an entry after that terrifying Sunday morning.

December 13th:

When I got my chemo bag off, I thought the side effects would start getting better. No one told me they would get worse. Sunday morning my mouth sores had gotten so unbearable, I was in tears. Phil had to leave to go to church, but I was scared to be alone. We called Melissa, and miraculously she was not at church, so she came and sat with me all day. We called the on-call doctor and got a prescription for numbing meds. It didn't help much. How I felt and what I knew to be true were at complete odds with each other. I kept trying to remind myself that the chemo was getting rid of the cancer, but I honestly felt that whole week like the chemo was killing me.

I still sense the same tears welling up inside when I look back at my words today. Only this time, they're tears of gratitude and joy. I see how, in the darkest times of treatment, God provided what we needed at the precise moment. How awesome our God is! I also see my husband's example of a pivotal truth that determines our ability to trust God through those dark times. To trust Him to be our provision, strength, or whatever we need. Our willingness to trade our *what-ifs* for *as-ifs*.

What Is a What-If?

If you've stuck with me this far, then what-ifs likely need no introduction. Because we get each other, you and me. Soul-sisters do that, you know. They get each other. Still, we need to pause for a quick second and get a clear definition of a *what-if* before moving forward. It's important for us to understand their origin in order to know how to manage them.

What-ifs are a side-effect of the worst-case-scenario mentality we learned about. When we come face-to-face with unexpected circumstances, we sense our self-sufficiency slipping away. We lose control, and that scares us. We want wisdom to be able to figure things out on our own and answer the what-if questions. What if it doesn't work out? What if something bad happens? What if God doesn't answer? Focusing on the unknown gives fear an edge. God wants us to release our need for answers to the what-ifs and trust Him completely.

Whatever our unique situation, we all know the unsettling feelings brought on by what-if questions. Jesus understood this. In Mark 9, he addresses our doubt in a conversation with a desperate father. Jesus helped him with his unbelief, and he does the same for us. In a guest post at kristinebrown.net, my friend Lyli Dunbar wrote about that story and how it relates to the what-ifs in our lives:

> "This morning, I turned to Mark 9 and read about the man who brought his mute son to Jesus. I picture this father carrying his boy with the foaming mouth to the Savior. I see his tiny frame twitching uncontrollably as his father stands there holding his body up as an offering. His father pleads for Jesus to have a heart and help his precious child who had endured uncontrollable convulsions day after day. This weighed down man holds up his son and says, "If you can do anything, do it."
>
> Jesus' response captured my attention: "If? There are no 'ifs' among believers. Anything can happen" (MARK 9:23 MSG). When we bend down and believe, our what-ifs turn into without a doubt."

Looking into the eyes of a desperate dad, Jesus offered the answer to every what-if question ever whispered. We win the battle with the what-ifs when we let them point us toward God's promises.

Letting a What-If Point Me to My Promise

A midnight panic session ensued, triggered by a barrage of what-ifs I'd entertained earlier in the day. Now frantic, I tried to think of verses that would help. But where to start? I needed specifics. I couldn't just open the Bible and hope for the best. I needed a *right-now* promise I could cling to in that desperate moment.

Like the man lifting his mute son to Jesus, I cried out for relief from the heaviness of not knowing what to do. I needed Jesus' peace to remind me; there are no what-ifs with God.

I had been reading my friend Micah Maddox's book, *Anchored In*, and the chapter called "Power in the Dark" came to mind right then. So I grabbed the book from the shelf and flipped to that chapter. This quote was the first thing I read, "Darkness is only a distraction. It does not mean God has departed."[20] As I scanned the pages, I came upon verse after verse about God's power and help in our most desperate times. Verses like this one:

"Yea, though I walk through the valley of the shadow of death, I will fear no evil: for thou art with me; thy rod and thy staff they comfort me" (PSALM 23:4 KJV).

I read each verse, and my heart calmed. I let out a deep breath, releasing any question about God's ability. Instead of giving what-if questions freedom to take over, I let them point me to promises straight from His Word. I chose to claim those promises for me as Truth.

Rahab's Right-Now Promise

Rahab's promise from the Lord came in the form of two messengers from Israel's camp. So we might wonder how she knew this was God's promise for her and her family. To find the answer, let's pause and put ourselves in her place. How did she know she could trust them? Assuring her of a rescue in the middle of battle seems pretty far-fetched. Especially since they didn't exactly have time to think it through. But there was something that drew Rahab to their words. Something that identified the spies' guarantee as a direct promise from God. It was a solution she could never have come up with on her own. The answer to her need *right now.*

God's timing is perfect, and it is also beyond our human capacity to understand. To see God's unmatched timing in action, we can go back in history to when Joshua first saw the Promised Land. Remember Joshua and Caleb's favorable report to Moses? The one we discovered in Chapter 2, leading us to a new revelation about Rahab's intel? She'd heard about God's promises fulfilled for His people her whole life. But maybe what she didn't know was how unfavorably the Israelites responded! Rather than charging forward to claim their promise, they grumbled and threatened their leaders. "But the whole community began to talk about stoning Joshua and Caleb" (Numbers 14:10a NLT).

That's when Aaron and Moses demonstrated one of the most powerful things we can do as God's children. They fell face-down and cried out, "Please, Lord, prove that your power is as great as you have claimed. *For you said...*" (NUMBERS 14:17 NLT, EMPHASIS MINE).

Even though the Israelites refused to accept the promise God offered, that didn't stop a faithful few from praying. Aaron and Moses cried out to their Lord what they knew to be true. They claimed the promise by reminding God what He had already said. Although it looked as if the plan was delayed, the leaders continued to live as if God wouldn't fail.

Identifying Our Promise

We know God is for us. We also know His Word is true. But in those desperate times—like my midnight panic session or fear-filled Sunday morning—we need help identifying our promise for the situation. And if it doesn't come in the form of two spies knocking at our door, how do we find it?

Rahab's ability to trust that the men would follow through on their word didn't begin that night. Her foundation—what she'd learned about the Lord's faithfulness—helped point her to her promise. She knew it in her heart when it presented itself because it lined up with God's character. She was familiar with His character because she'd immersed herself in stories of His wonder.

Still unclear about discovering the promise from God for what you're going through? Here are three things that will help us to identify our right-now promise.

First, immerse ourselves in God's Word. I'd like to think I spend plenty of time with my Bible. I read a devotion, check my verse-of-the-day, and follow inspirational speakers on social media. I even have favorite verses and quotes framed as artwork all around the house. But truthfully, it's easy to get into the habit of thinking I'm all good. That I'm doing all the Bible study I need to do. When I realized I'd been struggling to hear from the Lord, I decided I needed a change. I began praying for God to reveal creative ways for me to reconnect with His Word.

We serve a creative, inspiring God. He made you and me, after all! And when we ask, He will show us new ways to hear His Words come alive in a very personal way. If you've been in a similar habit and feel a deep longing to hear His voice more clearly, check out the "Applying It" section in the companion workbook. (You'll find the link at the back of this book.) In that guide, you'll find a list of creative ideas for immersing yourself in God's Word.

Second, have God's promises readily available. What a blessing to have Micah's book on my shelf, highlighted and tabbed with sticky notes. Ready when I needed help. As I prepared to write this book, I read several other books about trusting

God and relying on His promises. Then I realized how precious it was to have encouraging words close by, which inspired me to do the same for you. So I created the *Glossary of God's Promises* and added it to the back of this book.

The *Glossary of God's Promises* is a collection of verses I compiled over time. It's an alphabetical listing by topic, where you'll find verses for protection, comfort, healing, direction, and much more. I even left space at the end for you to add your own favorites. Accept this resource as a gift from me to you. A place to turn when you need to immerse yourself in His truths or hear His voice. I pray it becomes a go-to source of hope for you, my friend.

Third, believe what God says. Boy, do I crave control. Giving my problems to God is an everyday recommitment for me, because when I'm hit with unexpected challenges, I realize my own strength isn't enough. That's one reason we stay tied to the Verbal Level of trust. We love reading God's promises, but we stop short of doing the one thing Rahab demonstrated with such grace and resolve. We haven't said, "I believe," and meant it.

Believing that God will do what He says is tough for us go-getter girls. Our inner urge to figure things out can get in the way of the choice to believe. We can lay our burdens at the feet of Jesus over and over, but the only way we will move to that next trust level is by believing God can and God will.

Living As-If

Journal Entry January 21st:

It has been one month since I recorded anything here. The physical pain and exhaustion became too much to do anything except rest and force myself to eat. We found out as I neared the end of radiation treatments that I would be having 30, not 28, which I originally thought. Not welcome news, considering I couldn't sit, could barely walk, and still had unbearable pain. I had to press through and finish! I've had wonderful encouragers texting, calling, and sending gifts. Those gestures mean so much. I still find myself seeking God and wanting to understand more about what He wants me to learn through all this. I am actively practicing trusting Him in ALL things. I have purposefully not looked at the paper that tells the staging of the diagnosis. I am BELIEVING that God is healing me.

Cancer causes all kinds of what-ifs to surface. *What if we choose the wrong treatment path? What if the cancer spreads? What if treatments aren't successful? What if I can't survive this?* Even in recovery, every body ache can trigger a what-if question if I let it. Early in my cancer battle, my good friend and fellow writer Pam Stockdale sent me a list of her favorite Scriptures about healing. Knowing I would soon begin 30 rounds of radiation, I chose to meditate on one verse a day—one for each treatment. Focusing on

Scripture before facing radiation helped me trust Him even more with each passing treatment.

Even when the treatment plan resulted in a level of pain like I'd never fathomed, God's promises took me from the what-ifs to living as-if. As if God would see me through it. As if my trial was part of a bigger plan. As if the treatments would be successful.

When the what-ifs begin to surface, we can take action by shifting our perspective. In the chart below, I've given a few examples of trading your *what-ifs* for living *as-if.*

WHAT IF...	I will live AS IF...
things don't work out?	things will work out because God is in control.
something bad happens?	God will work everything together for my good.
I mess things up?	God takes our mistakes and turns them into lessons for our growth.
God doesn't answer my prayer?	God will answer in His timing.

Challenge yourself to define your own what-if/as-if transitions. Write them in the blank spaces in the chart. Then spend a few minutes sealing the chapter foundation principle on your heart.

I can leave what-ifs behind and live as-if God's Word is true, because it is.

The reality is that what-if questions will never go away. Our problem-solving minds will continue trying to figure things out on our own. The key is not to try to get rid of them, but to overcome them. So rather than letting them point us to fear, we can shift our *what-ifs* to living *as-if*.

Untying Old Habits

Dear Heavenly Father,

It seems like every day of my life is a battle against what-if questions. I know entertaining these thoughts isn't healthy, but I feel like I'm losing the fight. I turn to you in desperation, Lord. I can't silence all the what-ifs without your help.

Rahab knew her right-now promise, and she held onto that

promise even when her situation seemed hopeless. Help me have faith like Rahab and seek you for my right-now promise. Your Word is true, and your promises are sealed.

When I can't hear your voice, show me creative new ways to connect with you. Refresh my time in your Word and give me the wisdom to know you more. As I learn about your character, I can live as if your promises for me are yes and amen. Because they are. In Jesus' name, Amen.

Living It Out: Identifying Your Promise

Rahab's promise came right when she needed it, although it likely didn't look the way she expected. Our answers from God often will be more than our human minds can comprehend. That's why immersing ourselves in His Word and studying His truth for our lives will help us see the answer when it comes knocking at our door.

CHAPTER 7

Leaving the Knot Alone

HOW DO I RESIST HELPING GOD? WHEN
WAITING ON THE PROMISE LEADS TO DOUBT.

"Those who know your name trust in you, for you, O Lord, do not abandon those who search for you."

PSALM 9:10 NLT

Those of you who've known me for a while may recall me shar-ing about the ongoing parade of wildlife in my backyard. It's a saga I don't anticipate will end any time soon. Just when I make progress relocating one creature, another one finds shelter nestled in our overgrown shrubs and trees. Never a dull moment. Some are less welcome than others, if you catch my meaning. Birds are more pleasant than armadillos, and I'd choose a squirrel over a mole any day. But of all the animals traipsing through our back-yard, my favorite are the bunnies.

I can always count on our trusty dog Bandit to alert me to any new critters. But one particular day, his screeching bark pierced my ears more than usual. I ran to the yard to pull him away from whatever he'd found. That's when I discovered them. Little balls of soft fluff buried under a mound of dirt. Right smack in the middle of the fresh-cut grass! No shelter, no protection. A burrow of baby bunnies vulnerable to being dug up by an overzealous dog.

I had to do something! I couldn't leave them there; and to make matters worse, a storm was predicted to hit soon. How would they survive? I hustled inside and began researching online "what to do when you find baby bunnies in your yard." I didn't have a moment to lose. Those precious babies were counting on me. *Weren't they?*

I scoured wildlife websites, and article after article offered the same advice. If you find a burrow with baby rabbits, leave it alone. The mother will be back for them.

What? So I was supposed to forget about helping and leave them there, with a storm coming? I couldn't believe what I read. I sought out different sources to confirm but didn't find anything that advised, "Dig up those baby bunnies and bring them inside." Nope, nothing even remotely close. I had my answer. Now, I had to once again resist helping and trust God's plan.

For the next 24 hours (give or take a few), I sat within eyeshot of the back windows. I may have even scooted my chair a little to get a better view. I watched. I waited. When the storm came, everything inside me screamed to rescue the helpless creatures. But I'd learned from past experiences what happens when I intervene without God's go-ahead. Oh yes, I'd been in this place many times before. The place of waiting and resisting. I had to learn the hard way how to identify God's nudges and let Him handle it.

After the rain let up, I glanced again. To my great relief, a fully grown momma rabbit stood over the burrow. Little heads poked through the dirt for feeding time. God gave that momma everything she needed to take care of her young, and she didn't need my help to do it.

Help! I Need to Intervene

Resisting the urge to intervene doesn't come naturally for us go-getters. It takes practice. And in the case of the baby bunnies, my practice meant not moving from my chair. Sometimes it's hard to stay put and wait! Yet so often, that's exactly what God calls us to do. He has the plan worked out, and our interference can delay its fulfillment. "I wait for the Lord, my soul waits, and in his word I hope" (PSALM 130:5 ESV).

God had the plan worked out for Rahab too, and she knew not to interfere. No matter how long it took. Once Rahab cinched the cord to her window, she had quite the wait ahead of her. Time to sit inside her house. Do nothing. Oh, the agony! I, for one, would've tried to take matters into my own hands. Loosen the rope, maybe just a little. I could've sent a family member on a covert mission to see if anyone was coming. Or better yet, let the whole family down the same way I had sent the spies and run far away. My mind would go into hyperdrive developing one plan after another, until I'd either exhausted myself fretting over it or convinced myself they weren't coming back for us. But not Rahab. We can count on her to inspire us with her next-level kind of trust. The kind that strengthens us to wait well when we want to *do something*.

Let's visit Rahab again, right after she tied the red rope to her window. The next few verses and chapters describe a timeline of waiting for God's promise to be fulfilled.

Rahab's Waiting Timeline

The sounds of footsteps faded into the night as Rahab retreated, "leaving the scarlet rope hanging from the window" (JOSHUA 2:21B NLT). No need to wake the family at this hour. Dawn would come soon enough. Just like the spies' promised return, she could count on it.

Scripture doesn't show us the inside of Rahab's home during the wait. Instead, the perspective shifts to the happenings within the Israelite camp. Because of this accurate account of their steps toward victory, we also get a valuable lesson for our waiting seasons. Sometimes it takes a while for us to receive the promise.

"The spies went up into the hill country and stayed there three days. The men who were chasing them searched everywhere along the road, but they finally returned without success" (JOSHUA 2:22 NLT).

Urgency grew with every day the king's men failed to find the hidden spies. Thankfully the hills provided the deep cover they needed, and Rahab had given them good advice about staying put for three days. That proved to be the exact time frame before the soldiers gave up and returned to Jericho. This verse begins the recorded days from the tying of the cord to Rahab's pending rescue.

After three days, they made it across the river to give Joshua the fantastic news. "Then the two spies came down from the hill country, crossed the Jordan River, and reported to Joshua all that had happened to them. 'The Lord has given us the whole land,' they said, 'for all the people in the land are terrified of us.'" (JOSHUA 2:23-24 NLT).

Early the next morning, the quest began. But Joshua knew better than to get ahead of God. He would seek the Lord with every step, giving thanks and praise to Him for bringing them to this blessed place. They packed their tents and moved from Acacia Grove to the bank of the river, where they camped *three more days.* "Then Joshua told the people, "Purify yourselves, for tomorrow the Lord will do great wonders among you" (Joshua 3:5 NLT).

I love how God provided a chance for His people to rest before issuing the next step forward. A chance to wake up refreshed and ready to experience His blessings anew. There's something marvelous about mornings. God-given opportunities to start again. Scripture compares God's promises to dawn, like this word from the prophet Hosea, "Oh, that we might know the Lord! Let us press on to know Him. He will respond to us as surely as the arrival of dawn or the coming of rains in early spring" (Hosea 6:3 NLT).

The Israelites did press on. "The people crossed the Jordan on the tenth day of the first month. Then they camped at Gilgal, just east of Jericho" (Joshua 4:19 NLT). They built a memorial there so one day they could tell the rest of the story to their children. God didn't only deliver them from captivity; He delivered them to the Promised Land.

Then they camped at Gilgal that night.

Let's pause to take a peek through the window of Rahab's home right now. Remember, she and her relatives know nothing about what's going on down by the river. All they know is since Rahab told them to stay inside, they'd better listen.

Several days into the wait, Rahab's family had first-hand knowledge of what it was like to be stuck inside together. I wonder if the same tension built back then as sometimes does in our modern world? Uncle Lou or Aunt Bee getting on your nerves? You wouldn't even be able to take a walk outside to clear your head. I'm certain many of us can relate to their family's situation. Too much togetherness can cause a new level of irritation to form within the walls of an otherwise harmonious home. But I'm also certain, even without knowing all the details of the goings-on in Rahab's house, we can confirm this idea: *Rahab led by example.* She chose to rely on the presence of Almighty God.

So the next time family togetherness unleashes frustration in our homes, we can resolve the turmoil with unquestionable truth. The way to take control away from frustration is to pay more attention to God's presence than our feelings.

The camp at Gilgal...

Joshua circumcised the next generation of men. Their fathers had all been circumcised but had died during the 40 years of wilderness wandering. So before going any further, the covenant between God and His people would be renewed. How long did it take to complete the task itself? With 600,000 men? We can only speculate. After the procedure, however, tradition required the men to rest and heal for seven days.[21] While resting—four days after crossing—they celebrated Passover.[22] The very next morning, they enjoyed fresh bread made from the harvested land instead of the manna God had been providing for food.

Now, they were ready. No doubt Rahab was too. Remember, she's been staying inside the house with her family *this whole time.* Each dawn waking up wondering if today's the day. Holding onto hope's reminder in the certain sunrise. We may not be able to calculate an exact time, but with the addition of the famous Jericho march, we can make a pretty close guess. At least three to four weeks passed, maybe more. Plenty of time for worry, frustration, and doubt to come knocking at her heart's door. Would she cave to it or continue to trust?

"But those who wait for the Lord [who expect, look for, and hope in Him] Will gain new strength and renew their power; They will lift up their wings [and rise up close to God] like eagles [rising toward the sun]; They will run and not become weary, They will walk and not grow tired" (ISAIAH 40:31 AMP).

Linda's Story, in Her Own Words

"Trusting God with my circumstances has always been a problem. Only recently have I been beaten down so badly by events that I'm turning it ALL over to the Lord rather than falsely attempting my own solutions.

The incessant health problems that have left me unable to walk without assistance, coupled with incorrect diagnoses and many unsuccessful treatments, have left me floundering and hopeless for two years. My resentment of bad calls by medical providers has me questioning if even the Lord can dig me out from these frustrating, painful dilemmas.

I initially awake happy then remember: when I try to get out of bed and ambulate, I will hit that wall of pain and inability to fight back. Prayer gives me strength but knowing that nothing has changed leaves me hopeless. I usually go back to sleep rather than face defeat when I sit up and swing my legs over the side of the bed. Tears moisten my face in defeat.

I decided to change my approach. In addition to praying scripture before I have a chance to derail in the mornings, I speak to the Holy Spirit. Not that I'm cherry-picking the Trinity! I simply decided perhaps He'd appreciate me appreciating Him! After all, He's my Counselor and Advisor! I began to ask Him specifically for someone on earth to hear my pleas and try to guide me to someone who would champion my cause. I needed help! I turned it over to God, stopped the dozens of phone calls to try to find help on my own, and... waited. Friends and family were concerned that I'd given up. I explained that it was high time I turned this over to the Great Physician!

I went to an appointment to see my cardiologist. Just a checkup. She became so very concerned about the pain etched into my face and the downhill health status from a year ago that she picked up the phone and began shuffling my appointments for tests from months away to now and made them urgent! She spoke to the specialists I need to see before I undergo surgery. She was proactive and showed wonderful advocacy. These weren't her specialty areas, but she dove in and used her influence to help me get the appointments I'll need to proceed with care and treatment.

I hadn't trusted God with my circumstances. I know the medical system well from my ICU background. I couldn't navigate it any longer to help myself. I had to let it go. All I did was go to a scheduled appointment with a doctor who had nothing to do with my pain or treatment. If that wasn't the Holy Spirit at work, I don't know who else could have turned this mess around for me! This isn't about a cure. This is about finally setting aside my pride and trusting God. Now I awaken with hope for my future. It's in God's hands.

I've given up on God many times—in relationships, fears, broken heart, and disappointments in myself and others. I know better than to give up on Him. When we fall ALL of the way down to the depths of despair, we learn. How much better it is to ALWAYS trust Him to get it right? Certainly better than we can!"

I asked my community at **kristinebrown.net** to share their stories of trusting God through hard times, and the moment I read the email Linda sent, I knew I had to ask her if I could share it here with you. What an example of trusting God in times of waiting! When we have nothing to do but sit and wait on the promise, doubt comes searching for an open door. Waiting well means remaining in an attitude of total trust. Waiting well leaves no room for doubt. Our foundation principle is this:

Don't let your faith wane in the waiting. Keep trusting.

Rahab's future held hope too, along with generations to come. After her time of waiting, God made good on His promise to Rahab. The Israelites circled the walls of Jericho in silence. Seven more days. And in that magnificent moment when Joshua gave the order to move, he remembered Rahab.

"The seventh time around, as the priests sounded the long blast on their horns, Joshua commanded the people, "Shout! For the Lord has given you the town! Jericho and everything in it must be completely destroyed as an offering to the Lord. Only Rahab the prostitute and the others in her house will be spared, for she protected our spies" (JOSHUA 6:16-17 NLT).

Rahab's hope resided in trusting. She left the rope tied to her window for however long the wait. She refused to let go of the promise. From her time of waiting, we find inspiration for God's promises to be fulfilled in our own lives as well. Inspiration to help us wait well for days, weeks, or even years, when we're tempted to untie the rope and help God in our own strength.

Untying Old Habits

Dear Heavenly Father,

You are a God who has never failed me. Time and time again you've been faithful to keep your promises. Forgive me for struggling to trust you, especially in the waiting. I know your plan is perfect, and I can trust your Word no matter how long it takes.

Lord, I am sorry for trying to do things in my own strength when I get impatient. Help me resist the urge to intervene when you've made it clear I should trust you completely. Help me learn from Rahab how to wait well by refocusing each day on your promises for my life.

Thank you for being present with me and for working while I wait. In Jesus' name, Amen.

Living It Out:
Leave Your Knot Alone

Do you recall a time of waiting in your own life? A time when you wanted to help God? Maybe you're in a waiting season right now. If so, let our foundation principle settle into your heart. Keep trusting.

CHAPTER 8

Decision Stages

MAYBE THIS WASN'T SUCH A GOOD IDEA!

"Trust in the Lord with all your heart, And lean not on your own understanding; In all your ways acknowledge Him, And He shall direct your paths."

PROVERBS 3:5-6 NLT

Two Roads Diverged, or Three, or Four

I've read the iconic poem "The Road Not Taken" by Robert Frost at least a hundred times. Probably more.

That may sound like an exaggeration from this former English teacher, but trust me, it's the honest-to-goodness truth. Fifteen years in the classroom with junior high students and poetry curriculum gave me ample opportunities to ponder the ins and outs of Frost's famous lines, ending with this final stanza:

*"I shall be telling this with a sigh
Somewhere ages and ages hence:*

Two roads diverged in a wood, and I –
I took the one less traveled by,
And that has made all the difference."23

Taking time to research what people think about Frost's ideas, I found arguments about what the poem means. On the surface, it seems like an ode to not following the crowd. Doing something different, even when it's scary. But some disagree. There are two distinct schools of thought, one popular and the other more critical. Each of us may interpret it differently than the next person, and that's okay. Poetry can be subjective, after all. So for our purposes here, I'd like us to focus on one particular idea in the poem we can all agree on. Something Robert Frost gave no room for debate, and that is this. Ultimately, the man standing in the road would—at some point—have to choose.

How long did the man wait before deciding which road to take? Did he have a time limit? I can't help but wonder what he thought about while waiting. Because like Rahab's situation, waiting can allow for a whole lot of agonizing. Unless we are turning to the Holy Spirit for steadfast peace and keeping our confidence in God's power.

I catch myself giggling a little at the implication that there were only two roads in the story. Kind of like my pro and con lists I described earlier, my choice of direction looks more like the downtown Dallas mixmaster than a fork in the road. Still, I can totally see myself doing what the traveler did. Staring hard down one path, straining to see the end.

> "Two roads diverged in a yellow wood,
> And sorry I could not travel both
> And be one traveler, long I stood
> And *looked down one as far as I could...*"

Let's picture ourselves standing where these two roads diverged. What comes to mind for you as you gaze down each path? Do you stretch tall to see the horizon, or better yet, reach for your glasses? Or do you stay put until you get an inkling of which way to go? We learned in Chapter 2 how trusting God can calm the decision-making chaos. We also learned in Chapter 3 to trade our worst-case scenarios for drawing as close to Jesus as possible. I'd say we've come a long way, team. Just thinking about it excites me. We've learned to hold onto our unchanging God and do more than simply *say* we trust Him. We're doing it! Yet even with internalizing these truths, something about this crossroads moment still pulls at me. Something I noticed that has had a profound impact on my ability to trust.

Frost didn't write about turning back as an option.

Three roads—not two—led away from where he stood. One to the right, one to the left, and one in reverse. But nothing is mentioned of the road from where he came. So often I try to turn around and go back, try to undo my decision. And let me tell you, nothing good comes from that my friend. A whole lot of stress and worry instead of the peace and joy that's available to us. Which led me to discover a pattern in my life—one that's true for many. We can get wrapped up in what I like to call the decision stages. Once we're aware of how vulnerable we are to these stages, we can move forward with confidence and complete trust.

Decision Stages

When we attempt to tackle indecision ourselves rather than resting in God's guidance, we risk developing *decision fatigue*. This happens early in the decision-making process. Remember when Rahab responded with immediate obedience? Responding eases the burden of decision fatigue. But decision fatigue (also known as analysis paralysis) isn't the only stage of decision-making we need to watch out for. There are four other stages we may face when making decisions: *decision panic*, *decision regret*, *decision guilt*, and *decision reversal*. Knowing the signs of these potentially hazardous stages and what to do about them will help us see even more growth in our trust relationship with God.

1. DECISION PANIC.

Most decisions we make have some sort of deadline attached. Deciding whether to sign up our kids for little league means if we don't turn in the form and money by a certain date, they won't be allowed to play. When the boss extends that new job offer, we have to decide by a specific date, or they'll promote someone else. So in those days when the deadline draws closer and closer, we can fall victim to the grip of decision panic.

There's something frightening about deadlines. Knowing you must choose, or else! And the fact is, sometimes that panic can force us to make a decision without feeling peace about it. Panic is no joke. It can lead to heart, blood pressure, and a host of other physical issues. Yes, deadlines are a part of life. But panic does not have to accompany those last-minute decisions. Psalm 62:8 reads, "Trust in him at all times, you people; pour out your hearts to him, for God is our refuge" (NIV). When we pour out our hearts to God, He will guard us against the throes of decision panic. With power over the panic, we can stop fretting over what to do and live immersed in the peace in Jesus.

2. DECISION REGRET.

Sweet relief comes the instant a decision is made. Like the feeling of indulging in a hot fudge sundae to celebrate a special occasion, it soothes the spirit that suffered at the hands of decision panic for so long. It just feels good to have finality, to have the decision made. Unfortunately, that sweet relief may only last a brief moment before the next stage begins—decision regret. Decision regret can happen right after enjoying that delectable sundae. It looks something like this:

- You call your boss and accept the new job offer, but the minute you end the conversation, a sick feeling sinks into your stomach. You regret the decision and consider calling her back.

- You enroll your child in public school after years of homeschooling, but when day one comes, you can't relax, wondering if she's going to be okay.

- Your decision to move your parents to a facility where they can get better care weighs on you each night. Did you do the right thing? Or will the move be too hard on them?

Decision regret brings the illusion that we would've been happier if we'd taken a different path or made another choice. Especially when things don't turn out the way we planned. Sister, imagine me reaching right through this book and grabbing your hand across the table as I say this. Decision regret and I are long-time acquaintances. Because I know it so well, you can believe this tidbit of tough love comes straight from my personal playbook. Regret is not from God. Many times I've thought to myself, "If only I'd chosen differently, none of this would've happened." Only I'd failed to see that maybe things were exactly the way God planned. Maybe He intended to use what I was going through for my ultimate good.

Everything that comes from God is good, even the hard things. Because He works all things together for what's best for us. But regret is an evil foe. It wants nothing more than for us to walk around with heaviness in our spirits, refusing to move forward because the weight is too much. That's why we need to have a clear understanding of decision regret right now. When we see it for what it is, we will recognize it when it tiptoes into our lives. The psalmist wrote in Psalm 73:24, "You guide me with your counsel, and afterward you will receive me to glory" (ESV).

Are you lingering under a cloud of decision regret right now? If so, pause and breathe in. As you exhale, read the verse above and let it soothe you and bring clarity. I pray God will speak to you about your need and free you from all the "if only" thoughts keeping you bound. If we know God is guiding us, we have every right to leave regret on the table right beside that empty bowl of deliciousness we just consumed.

3. DECISION GUILT.

When my son grew into a young adult, the fears I had convinced myself were irrational became all too real when I missed several middle-of-church phone calls from 1500 miles away. I hadn't stepped in when his mission team set out on a cross-country trip toward a potential snowstorm. They had already traveled halfway to their destination when my son informed me they'd set a new course several states away to help out at a ministry event in New York. Although every mom-instinct inside me screamed *no*, I had to trust that God would protect them. That meant continuing to trust, even when while serving at the event, my boy landed in the emergency room with stitches from a near-fatal mishap.

You'd better believe my first reaction sent me searching for any possible way to get there, but being in the midst of a cancer battle meant I had to stay put. There's nothing quite like the heartache distance creates when a loved one needs us. God in his grace and mercy surrounded our son with level-headed people to get him the help he needed and be there when I couldn't. That left me confined at home with a choice to make. I could respond in a frantic attempt to ease my own guilt over my decision to let him go on the trip, or I could respond Rahab's way. I could walk in instant obedience. In this situation, my instant obedience meant praying for God's provision and resting in His goodness.

Trusting God to take care of our families can be hard. Boy, can we heap that guilt on ourselves when something bad happens! I could've very well blamed myself for not intervening and keeping my boy in a bubble of protection I'd built, even with the added unexpected surgery in the weeks following the accident. Instead, I chose to praise God for bringing him through the ordeal and teaching us both more about trust in the process.

There are times when all we can do is pray the words of Psalm 84:12, "Lord Almighty, blessed is the one who trusts in you" (NIV). When I noticed call after call in my voicemail that Sunday after church, I knew it had to be bad news. There was no way I could've possibly helped from so far away, but I also knew this: I had prayed, so I decided to trust God over wallowing in the guilt of feeling responsible. God did not create us to carry guilt for our actions, including past decisions made. He created us to carry them to Christ.

4. DECISION REVERSAL.

Probably the most painful stage of all, decision reversal entertains the question "Did I hear God wrong?" It allows the step of faith to be overrun by second-guessing, sending us running back toward the safety of our comfy couch. It means we gave in to the what-ifs, tucked our boldness away for safe-keeping, and changed our minds. Now let me be clear, sometimes backing out on a decision is wise. When we've prayed and don't feel peace about our decision, God could be pointing us toward a different road. Or sometimes, we just plain make a mistake in our decision, and that's okay. It happens. That's why daily giving control to God is so important. We may not always hear God's voice telling us what to do, which introduces our foundation principle for this chapter:

If we've asked the Holy Spirit to guide us, we need to trust that He's doing it.

"I will instruct you and teach you in the way you should go; I will counsel you with my loving eye on you" (PSALM 32:8 NIV). I'm so glad we serve a God of love, patience, and forgiveness. To list all the times I made a decision then changed paths would take an entire chapter! Yet every time, God protected me from harm and continued guiding me. At times I learned hard lessons but was always surrounded by His gentleness. He never gives up on us. So like me, if you've entertained a few decision reversals, only to find out you let second-guessing get the upper hand, it's not too late to start again. In her post *7 Keys to Trusting God's Plan for Your Life*, prayer writer Kathryn Shirey puts it this way, "Through the highs and in the lows, I've learned to trust God's plans for my life. It hasn't been an easy road – trusting God never is. It hasn't been quick—definitely not on any timeframe I've set over the years. The journey hasn't looked anything like what I thought it would. Yet, God's plan is always perfect and always right on time."[24]

Overcoming the Decision Stages

"Whether you turn to the right or to the left, your ears will hear a voice behind you, saying, 'This is the way; walk in it'" (ISAIAH 30:21 NIV).

As we think about each possible stage of decision-making, we may be tempted to believe true joy won't be a reality unless we defeat decision fatigue, panic, guilt, regret, and reversal. Allow me to serve up a heaping scoop of reassurance today. Let's replace the word *defeating* with *overcoming*. Decision stages will happen, and victory will come by working through them with purpose and determination. We can have that sundae with extra fudge and move forward in freedom. We may not be able to remove the decision stages from our lives for good, but we can overcome them with God's help. When we find ourselves in that familiar place, looking at the two, three, or four paths ahead, let's remember Rahab and praise God that we're becoming better deciders.

Did Rahab face the challenges of wanting to do what was best for her family? Had she overcome any decision stages as she demonstrated complete trust? I love how Rahab asked for a guarantee for her family, acting on the truth of God's promise for their rescue. But even more, I love that her trust in the One powerful enough to save them would not shift. With roads diverging before her in every direction, she chose the one that held the promise. And she would soon find out, that choice would mean everything.

Rahab gazed down the road ahead of her, but she didn't have to stretch tall to view what was coming. She could see the answer headed her way as marchers circled the city. The promise would soon arrive! She'd trusted, waited, prayed, and believed. But just before her promise became a reality, her world literally started to crumble.

Untying Old Habits

Dear Heavenly Father,

Thank you for your love, patience, and forgiveness. I am inspired by the stories of women who demonstrate how to live guided by the Holy Spirit, even in their most desperate times. I want to live like that, Lord. I want to live so aware of your guidance that I'm able to release the second-guessing, guilt, or regret of my choices.

I have struggled in the past with allowing my thoughts to get distracted by the decision stages. Thank you for showing me where I can continue to grow in my knowledge of your Word and how to listen for your instruction. I can see how far I've come in my journey to trust you on a new level. I am living out the trust I claim to know, and I give you all the praise!

God, you created all things, know all things, and work every-thing together for my good. I know you are with me. I can trust in that. In those times when I can't hear your Voice or sense you telling me which path to take, I will continue to trust and follow you in faith. In Jesus' name, Amen.

Living It Out: Where Roads Diverge

Tricia's Story…

She sat inside this painfully familiar place, desperate to break free from the addiction that overpowered her. She didn't want to be there. She had just found out what should've been welcome news. She was pregnant. But her addiction had such a hold on her, Tricia didn't think she could find the strength to get clean.

She noticed a man pacing outside the house. He seemed out of place. Drawn to him, she felt compelled to ask him what he was doing. Why was he there? He explained that he'd been given a new job opportunity and marching around the outside of the drug house reminded him how much the job meant to him. That if he wanted to keep his new job, he couldn't go into the house. No matter what. The job meant more to him than the drugs. Tricia longed to find that kind of strength. She wanted a new life for her and her baby. Then the man asked a question that altered Tricia's path forever. "You have to decide. Which do you love more, your baby or the drugs?"

As she drove away from her past that day and toward the future she hoped for, she cried out to God in her car. Her world was crumbling, but God met her there. Tricia explained how that day, God removed her desire to ever pick up drugs again. The urges were completely gone.

Now years later and still guided by the power of the Holy Spirit, Tricia often thinks back about that time. Sometimes she senses guilt and regret over her past addiction. So when those thoughts surface, she reminds herself who she is in Christ. Her love for God, her family, and others is an inspiration to me and all who know her.

Think of a time in your life when you experienced panic, regret, or guilt over a decision you made. Or maybe you reversed your decision because you questioned whether you heard God right. Take time right now to talk to God about that experience. What do you sense Him saying to you? Let God's love, patience, and forgiveness flow into your heart and refresh you right now. He is with you. Trust in that.

CHAPTER 9

When Your World Is Crumbling Around You

WILL THINGS EVER GET BETTER?

"I know the Lord is always with me. I will not be shaken, for he is right beside me."

PSALM 16:8 NLT

Carolyn's Story

It began like any other run to Walmart. Being a mom with three kids meant taking frequent trips to the store. Carolyn went about her shopping, faithfully displaying her cross necklace as she did every day, an effort to show her husband and everyone she knew that she believed. She couldn't have known a simple mishap would usher her into a journey of trusting God like never before.

She leaned over, snagging the necklace on her shopping cart. It broke. Carolyn remembers thinking, "Lord, how will people know I'm a Christian?" And with that simple question, she heard God answer.

"They will know you follow me because of your actions."

Soon that willingness to display her trust in God would be tested. Her husband's job moved to an overseas position, leaving them jobless. Carolyn's world began to crumble, yet she recalls looking up toward the mountains surrounding their home and praising God. James 1 became a huge God-promise for her—one she was determined to hold on to. "Consider it pure joy, my brothers and sisters, whenever you face trials of many kinds, because you know that the testing of your faith produces perseverance" (JAMES 1:2-3 NIV). Would she be able to persevere through this? Would her husband see her faith displayed when circumstances seemed hopeless?

Carolyn cinched her rope to God's guarantee. She prayed. She kept her mind focused on hearing from the Father. She sensed Him directing her to get the house in order, beginning with cleaning the garage. Three times she felt compelled to clean, organize, and sort the garage! And sure enough, after a series of miscommunications with the landlord, their house was sold out from under them. They were evicted on Mother's Day. Three kids, three dogs, jobless, and homeless. Yet her faith didn't waver.

They had three days to pack and move. Looking back now, Carolyn can see how God's promises for her and her family were revealed through their circumstances. If she hadn't responded to the Holy Spirit prompting her to clean the garage out, they wouldn't have been able to pack it all in those three days. The cross-state move took them to Colorado for a time and eventually landed them in Texas, where Carolyn and I met and became friends. Because of these God-inspired events in her life, I'm able to share her story with you here.

With her world falling apart, God fulfilled His promise. I will always remember this quote as Carolyn told me her story of trusting God. Through it all, she learned to "Praise God for closed doors!" Her husband came to faith in Jesus Christ, and they have both grown in their trust in God's power to provide.

Carolyn's story offers an example of a valuable truth. One Rahab also knew. Our circumstances don't reveal the full measure of God's plan. We can be fooled by what's going on around us unless we've built our shelter on trusting God to do what He says He will do. That's why it was so important for us to determine our trust level early in our journey and keep building with each new foundation principle. By looking back, we can see the progression of a strong foundation built on trusting God's Word. Let's look at the next foundation piece, then view it from Rahab's perspective.

We can be deceived by our crumbling circumstances unless we've built our foundation on trusting God.

Where the Rock Meets the Road

"When the people heard the sound of the rams' horns, they shouted as loud as they could. Suddenly, *the walls of Jericho collapsed*, and the Israelites charged straight into the town and captured it" (JOSHUA 6:20 NLT EMPHASIS MINE).

Was Rahab still peering out the window when the first rock fell? Did she freeze, confused by the deafening voices of God's people? Or did she gather her family in a corner and huddle over them with outstretched arms? Her imagined rescue surely leaned toward a different scene than this. As she'd watched the even-paced steps of the Israelites for seven days straight, she anticipated her long wait would soon see a great reward. *Seven days*. But this? Not at all what she expected.

One piece, then another—mud brick cracked and broke away from the ceiling. Bits of rock hit the floor of Rahab's home like rain pelting the flat roof. Only this rain could very well bring about her total destruction. Her entire body shook. Maybe because of the wall she pressed against in an attempt to brace herself, or maybe it was every nerve in her being trying in anguish to make it through whatever this was.

The Israelites' shouts faded into screams from the townspeople. Bricks collapsed all around Rahab and her family, then stillness. Somehow her home had survived. It had to be a miracle![25] A covenant God showing once again His true nature—faithful protector. No way she would have predicted this to be God's answer for her plea.

"Meanwhile, Joshua said to the two spies, "Keep your promise. Go to the prostitute's house and bring her out, along with all her family" (JOSHUA 6:22 NLT).

The sounds of soldiers climbing mounds of brick around her crumbled world brought an unlikely peace. Looking around at the circumstances, no one would believe they'd find anyone alive amid the mess. But they did.[26] There, just behind the red rope Rahab fixed to her window, and just as securely to her spirit.

"The men who had been spies went in and brought out Rahab, her father, mother, brothers, and all the other relatives who were with her. They moved her whole family to a safe place near the camp of Israel" (JOSHUA 6:23 NLT).

"In his hand are the depths of the earth, and the mountain peaks belong to him. The sea is his, for he made it, and his hands formed the dry land" (PSALM 95:4-5 NIV).

It's a hard concept for us to fathom—that the God who created the universe also cares about you and me. He is present in our daily lives and aware of every hard thing we go through. This Healer and Deliverer "...who created the heavens and stretched them out, who spread out the earth and what comes from it..." also provides exactly what we need when we need it (ISAIAH 42:5 ESV).

God shook the walls of Jericho that day. He did it for Joshua. He did it for Rahab. And he did it for countless others He knew by name and cared for more than anything else in existence. Are your walls shaking today? If so, I have earth-settling news. God cares for you, too. Let's look at a short but power-packed verse that can help us grasp the hope we struggle to see.

Living by Believing

A visit to the surgeon would let me know how well chemotherapy and radiation treatments worked and what surgery would be needed to finish wiping out the cancer. So I waited. Six long weeks of nothing but resting and recuperating gave my mind plenty of opportunities for doubt to come knocking. It took a targeted effort to redirect my thoughts back to God's promise. I thought about how God showed His power time and time again in my own circumstances. Recalling God's faithfulness helped me accept His peace and keep trusting.

Once again my husband and I sat in the exam room, prepared to hear the follow-up report. This room had become too familiar for comfort. My skilled surgeon didn't waste time delivering the news. He told me that when he first examined the area, he didn't like what he saw. So, he took several biopsies to be sure. But contrary to what he observed, every biopsy came back with this result: benign. No indication of cancer present.

Just like the mangled ruins of Jericho, no one would believe "good cells" could still be living among the mess inside my body. But God doesn't respond to us according to the happenings all around us. He responds according to His eternal plan.

I'd read a verse in recent weeks that came to my mind as I thought about the doctor's report. "For we live by faith, not by sight" (2 CORINTHIANS 5:7 NIV). So many instances in my life, I had trusted what circumstances looked like rather than God's infallible Word. I'd looked around and concluded nothing but hopelessness. "What's the use? This will never work." With each gloomy outlook, I unknowingly sealed my trust to a future doomed to fail. Now that pattern would end for me—God proved without a doubt the power of living by believing in Him, not by our situation. Because even though the word "benign" should have brought complete relief, my doctor still wanted me to consider removing the entire area. Going ahead with the extensive surgery could also remove any lingering doubt. Once again, I would have to choose.

We become vulnerable to worry, doubt, and indecision when we focus on what we see instead of what we believe. A wayward child may continue on a destructive path even though we commit to pray every day. Physical pain can increase even when our church prayer team intercedes for us at their weekly prayer meeting. The New Living Translation of 2 Corinthians 5:7 reads, "For we live by believing and not by seeing." Trusting that God is still moving us toward the promise means not focusing on what we see going on around us but what His Word says. As we've learned, things like frustration and waiting can make that hard to do. Daily irritations will happen. But when we live by believing and not by seeing, we show a level of faith that brings us closer to Jesus, our living hope.

When the Earth Quakes

Think about the most difficult situation you've ever encountered. It could be you're experiencing it right now as we journey together. Or maybe it's a memory you push aside anytime your mind attempts to go there because you'd much rather forget. But I'm asking you to count on me as we go to that place when your world crumbled too. It's important we visit it from a different viewpoint than before. To see the reality amid the pain—that sometimes God allows the earthquakes to come. "When the earth quakes and its people live in turmoil, I am the one who keeps its foundations firm" (PSALM 75:3 NLT).

When I'm going through the toughest battles of my life, I don't want to hear that "God has a plan for all this." I want relief for the moment. I need a reprieve, and I can't think beyond today to what good might come out of my trials later on. Right smack in the middle of the bad stuff, it's hard to fathom that this may be part of a bigger plan.[27]

As our worlds fall apart, all we can see is the evidence of the destruction. Our holy God may not reveal the *good* until later, when things quiet down and we sit in stunned silence in the aftermath. As we take a look back at our own earthquakes, it is then we can see God with us through it. We also discover the blessings that come after.

Yes, I said blessings.

One of the most treacherous things I recall from my cancer journey is knowing friends who also battled cancer but did not survive. People I loved who had been given similar diagnoses as me. My heart was tied in conflicting knots. As I thanked God for my healing, I also made plans to attend funerals.

How do we work through that? How do we find any good in the hurting or come to terms with things if God doesn't answer a prayer the way we want?

First, let's free ourselves from the pressure of thinking we need to rush through our pain. Feelings are created by God and given so that we can fully embrace the love and mercy He offers. So if someone approaches you right smack in the middle of heartache and proceeds to inform you that "God will bring something good out of this," you have my permission to ignore them for the moment. Even though their advice may be true, there is a time for it. Let yourself cry, friend. Or scream. Or hurt for a while. The key to finding the good in the hard is not pushing away the pain. It's trusting God to stay with you all the way through it.

"In you, Lord my God, I put my trust. I trust in you; do not let me be put to shame, nor let my enemies triumph over me" (PSALM 25:1-2 NIV).

Can you imagine how hard it was for Rahab to still believe with the walls that held her home in place falling in pieces? Just when she'd survived the waiting and spotted the promise coming her way? Surely she felt like peace and rest were finally within her reach. Like Rahab, you may have been in that place. When you welcome a sense of normalcy back into your life and feel like you're standing on firm footing once again. Then out of nowhere—bam! Things get crazy in the worst way. Or like my friend Carolyn, you may only see mountains surrounding you yet choose to hold on, knowing things are about to come crashing in.

The point we need to glean is that God came back for Rahab *in the middle of all the destruction.* Not after the rubble was cleared away and her situation started looking better. That's how His goodness manifests in our lives, as well. (Now, ready for the tell-it-like-it-is part?) We won't recognize the promise when it comes if we aren't consistently claiming the truth of Scripture as ours.

This is where the *rock* meets the road in our trust-life. Remember, our circumstances don't show us the fullness of God's plan. We can be fooled by what's going on around us unless we've built our lives on trusting God. Today let's commit to believing not according to our current struggles but according to God's perfect Word. To live by believing, not by seeing. Our understanding will reach beyond the immediate mess into eternal hope.

"So Joshua spared Rahab the prostitute and her relatives who were with her in the house, because she had hidden the spies Joshua sent to Jericho. And she lives among the Israelites to this day" (JOSHUA 6:25 NLT).

Untying Old Habits

Dear Heavenly Father,

Many times in life, I can't find hope in my situation or see beyond the turmoil surrounding me. All I feel is my world crumbling, and I struggle to hold onto your promise to come through for me. The truth of 2 Corinthians 5:7 gives me fresh hope today as I'm reminded, "For we live by believing and not by seeing" (NLT).

Thank you, Lord, for showing me in Rahab's story how your promise often comes in the middle of the destruction, not when things look like they're getting better. When everything seems to be falling apart, I will take a deep breath, turn to your Word, and accept the peace you give. When doubt tries to find an open door and make its way into my mind and heart, bring this verse to my remembrance. Teach me to focus not on my circumstances but on you alone. In Jesus' name, Amen.

Living It Out:
Is Your World Crumbling?

We have been encouraged by Carolyn's story to find one simple verse that is fitting to our situation and keep it at the center of our focus. Carolyn's verse that brought hope through her time of homelessness, unemployment, and uncertainty was this:

"Consider it pure joy, my brothers and sisters, whenever you face trials of many kinds, because you know that the testing of your faith produces perseverance" (JAMES 1:2-3 NIV).

As you pray, what is one verse God brings to mind that you can apply to your current circumstances? Do you have a go-to verse to help you through difficult times? Use the Glossary of God's Promises in the back of this book to find a verse that speaks to your heart in a special way today.

CHAPTER 10

Standing Firm in the River of Daily Demands

HOW TO NOT GET SWEPT AWAY WHEN THE
CURRENT STARTS RUSHING AGAIN.

"I pray that God, the source of hope, will fill you completely with joy and peace because you trust in him. Then you will overflow with confident hope through the power of the Holy Spirit."

ROMANS 15:13 NLT

God at the Center

"Look, the Ark of the Covenant, which belongs to the Lord of the whole earth, will lead you across the Jordan River!" (JOSHUA 3:11 NLT).

We've journeyed far from where we started, my friend. Not only recognizing what it takes to stay in steadfast trust, but to move forward without slacking. We've accepted these lessons from Rahab with a willingness to do what it takes to put them into action. We now understand how to keep God ever-present in our homes, relationships, and through hard things. But Rahab wasn't the only one in the story getting a tangible lesson. The Israelites saw first-hand the power of keeping God at the center.

I'm reluctant to backtrack since we've come so far. By now you know how much I enjoy forging ahead! However, our final lesson from Rahab's life rewinds a bit, to right before the nation of Israel crossed the river. Our final foundation principle can be found there. And since it's vital to our understanding, it's worth the brief detour. Joshua had just paused for a conversation with the Lord. Before each step, Joshua took a moment to ensure he made the next right move. (Anyone else feel a Holy Spirit nudge with that image?) He knew first-hand what could happen if they got ahead of God's plan. God gave Joshua specific directions to relay to the people, which began with getting the Ark of the Covenant set in place first.

"The priests will carry the Ark of the Lord, the Lord of all the earth. As soon as their feet touch the water, the flow of water will be cut off upstream, and the river will stand up like a wall" (Joshua 3:13 NLT).

God promised to part the waters! One more undeniable miracle to add to those we've witnessed. Like the widow's oil filled to overflowing, the Jordan River spilled over the banks. "But as soon as the feet of the priests who were carrying the Ark touched the water at the river's edge, the water above that point began backing up a great distance away at a town called Adam, which is near Zarethan. And the water below that point flowed on to the Dead Sea until the riverbed was dry" (JOSHUA 3:15B-16A NLT).

God made a way for his children to cross the river on dry ground as long as they kept the Ark of the Covenant at the center. I'll bet a few of them hesitated, looking out over the vast river. Israel had a notorious history of questioning God. Did they trust the One who brought them this far as they dipped a toe in the water? Whether reluctant or not, God made the way perfectly possible. His instruction for the priests to hold still in the middle demonstrated how He called them to live. The Ark symbolized God's presence. Just as Israel needed to keep Him at the center, we too need God's presence in the center of our lives every day.

On Firm-Footing

"The priests who were carrying the Ark stood in the middle of the river until all of the Lord's commands that Moses had given to Joshua were carried out. Meanwhile, the people hurried across the riverbed" (JOSHUA 4:10 NLT).

My family has embarked on more road trips across the southern US than I can count. On these back-and-forth highway adventures to visit relatives in other states, the single most stunning view is the Mississippi River. Whatever might be pulling our attention away from God's gorgeous creation, we always pause to check out the Mighty Mississippi. Sometimes the water levels appear low from our vantage point. Other times levels rise, making it appear even more powerful.

I've never been one to tackle a river rafting trip somewhere like Colorado or Arizona. I applaud anyone brave enough to try such a thing. (Not for me, thank you.) The extent of my river knowledge amounts to a scenic view or what I see in movies. Ever watched the scene from the film *Homeward Bound* when Sassy the cat slips while crossing a creek, sending her paddling helplessly downstream until her trusty sidekick Shadow comes to her rescue? I cover my eyes every time.[28] That's enough for me to swear off any river trips, other than maybe a lazy river ride at the local water park. But whether we've experienced the overpowering nature of rivers up close, in movies, or while driving across a bridge, we can all agree. There's unmistakable force in the current.

Life can be a lot like a river— sometimes crystal clear and calmly drifting in the direction of hope. Other times waters rise, multiplying the force of the current. Forceful enough to sweep our feet out from under us without warning. When waters rage, we are in danger of getting carried away as we struggle to get on firm footing again.

A few extra things on our to-do lists seem innocent enough, but add them up and you have the potential for disaster. We think we're standing strong one minute, and the next, we're straining to stay afloat. This is where the story of the Ark held in place holds such meaning in our own journeys. Because sometimes waters *will* rise. We've all felt it, but we can also count on this. Our Almighty God is the only one powerful enough to stop the force of a raging river.

"Yours, O Lord, is the greatness, the power, the glory, the victory, and the majesty" (1 CHRONICLES 29:11A NLT).

Bracing Ourselves for the Rush

As long as the Ark remained in place, the waters stopped flowing. But what happens in our circumstances when the river starts flowing again? When the waters rush, will we be able to keep steadfast trust in God?

"As soon as the priests carrying the Ark of the Lord's Covenant came up out of the riverbed and their feet were on high ground, the water of the Jordan returned and overflowed its banks as before" (JOSHUA 4:18 NLT).

Many of my darkest days fighting cancer, I found solace in quiet moments with the Lord. Conversations we had in the stillness of my bed, the room illuminated by the soft glow of a bedside lamp. I discovered such peace there. A peace that only came once I felt forced to stop the rush of life. To focus. To listen. God and I had some good talks, and I wanted them to continue long after I was healed and whole and back to my old self again. In fact, I didn't want to be my *old self.* I longed to be a newer, more grateful, more compassionate version of myself. Someone who stays present for her people, listens well, and lets things go.

There's something about a diagnosis that will prompt you to reevaluate things. And believe me, I had a lot to bring to the discussion. True to God's patient nature, He showed me how the seemingly innocent demands of my daily schedule overloaded me. How feeling frazzled all the time took my energy and attention. I realized in our one-on-one chats that it's impossible to overflow with hope when your life is overloaded with tasks. I needed a serious priority shift.

In the past I've had the best intentions when it came to my faith-walk. Yes ma'am, I've made more promises to God than I can count. What I learned from my friend Rahab is all about *His promises*, not mine. You see, we can be honestly, truly, one hundred percent thankful for God's blessings and honestly, truly, one hundred percent willing to trust Him in all things. We can build our foundation of faith in God and make a decision to keep it that way. But our good intentions won't protect us from the rising waters of life. Only God can. So to steady ourselves and keep living in this next-level kind of trust, we must prioritize our time with Him.

In her book, *More of God: A Distracted Woman's Guide to More Meaningful Quiet Time*, my friend Betsy de Cruz shares this scenario:

"On Sunday morning I hear an encouraging message or experience God touching my heart and meeting my needs during worship, but my joy bubble bursts when my kids start complaining in the car after we drive out of the church parking lot. My faith falls flat on Friday when our refrigerator breaks down just after we finish paying the fifth medical bill of the month. While I may not be rocking the church lady thing, I am learning to open the door of my heart to more of God. Because only God can grow my faith, give me the strength I need, and increase my joy."[29]

Maybe you can relate to Betsy's experience. You may also be wondering why I chose to rewind our story when we should be celebrating! Not only knowing God is trustworthy and saying we trust Him, but acting on what we know. Sister, we *are* in celebration mode. (Right now I'm savoring a delectable chocolate caramel in your honor.) But I'm also taking a cue from Rahab and anticipating the future. Because to move forward in victory, we need to brace ourselves in God's presence. Rahab's life lessons led us this far. It's time for us to take hold of the rope and carry on.

Carrying Confident Hope Forward

God continues to restore my health day by day. Sure, some days are better than others, but I watch in awe as his miracle gift unfolds one step at a time. I'm thankful the progress has been steady and ongoing. Because actually, I've wondered about my ability to stay in this place—living out trust in my everyday life. Will I fall back into a pattern of stress, worry, and frustration? Will I allow the demands of life to take over again? In her book *Breaking Anxiety's Grip*, Dr. Michelle Bengston says: "My attempts to fully trust God have been a tug-of-war. Sometimes I trust him so easily. Other times I fight with all my might trying to achieve in my own strength rather than trusting his. God isn't interested in fighting a battle to persuade us to trust him. He gave us all the reasons in his Word for us to trust him. Now he patiently waits for us to respond."[30]

Let's cinch this final foundation principle to our spirits, fellow traveler.

When life brings a rush of challenges, we can still overflow with hope by keeping God at the center.

Actively trusting God in every aspect of our lives brings with it the gifts of joy, peace, and confident hope.

We started weaving our stories together in chapter one with Romans 15:13. Now let's see how this miracle works. "I pray that God, the source of hope, will fill you completely with joy and peace *because you trust in him.* Then you will overflow with confident hope through the power of the Holy Spirit" (NLT, EMPHASIS MINE). When we trust God, He fills us with unending joy and peace. Hallelujah! And as we live filled up with that joy and peace, we will overflow with confident hope. Naturally, whatever overflows from us will spill out.

Author and speaker Jonita Mullins explains this concept beautifully by describing our lives like a filled bucket, that when jostled around, will spill out on those around us. Jonita writes in her newsletter, "If the water (in the bucket) was sweet, then that is what would spill out; if bitter, then that would overflow your bucket. This is true of our lives as well. As we walk along through life, we are jostled by people and problems. If we are full of anger, a bad temper or an ugly disposition, then that is what will spill out on those around us. But if we are filled with the abundant life of God then a smile, a sweet spirit and gentle words will come forth."[31]

I remember a time or two when my bucket spilled some nasty mess on those around me. But what an awesome promise we have in Romans 15:13—that all we need to do is trust Him, and the hope of Christ will be what pours out.

So as we turn the page on our time with Rahab and prepare to tie up loose ends, let's keep celebrating. God cares about everything from our biggest problem to the smallest details of our day. He doesn't expect us to go it alone. He is calling us to trust. He brought us this far, and He is still making the way perfectly possible.

Get ready to dip those toes in the water, precious child of God. Our daily lives will bring a rush of challenges our way. As long as we keep God placed firmly in the center, we have hope with each new day.

Untying Old Habits

Dear Heavenly Father,

Thank you for walking with me on this journey to trust you more. Thank you for the truths you've shown me from your Word and Rahab's story. I rejoice today that I'm leaning on you in times of worry, doubt, or frustration. I am turning to you when tough decisions must be made. You are my ever-present help, and "in your presence there is fullness of joy" (PSALM 16:11 ESV).

Lord, I want to stay in this new level of trust, and I know that means keeping you at the center of my life. When distractions and demands threaten to pull me under, fill me with your joy and peace as I trust in you. You are the only One powerful enough to sustain me when the river of life rages.

You are my shelter, my strong tower, and my hope. I declare to-day that you will remain at the center of my life, my home, and my family. I will forever rest in the assurance of your presence. In Jesus' name I pray, Amen.

Living It Out:
Don't Get Swept Away

God directed Joshua to send the priests into the Jordan River ahead of the people, carrying the Ark of the Covenant. As long as they held the Ark in the center, the waters stayed back. Once the Israelites crossed safely, the waters would flow again.

A raging current can throw us off balance, but keeping God at the center will help us when waters rage. Now that you've moved to a new level of trust in God, what daily demands threaten to pull your feet out from under you? How can you keep God placed firmly in the center of your life?

CHAPTER 11

Tying Up Loose Ends

ENJOYING A LIFE OF NEWFOUND TRUST.

*"But blessed are those who trust in the Lord and have
made the Lord their hope and confidence."*

JEREMIAH 17:7 NLT

A social media post I shared shortly after regaining my footing:

*"I did something amazing today, and I want to share it with
you. I went to Walmart. All by myself, and it was awesome.*

*Because when you can't go to Walmart all by yourself, you learn
to appreciate it. Cancer treatment changes your perspective like
that. About Walmart, and so much more. About. Absolutely.
Everything.*

*It also helped open my eyes to those of you who aren't able to go
to Walmart by yourself today, and I am truly sorry that I didn't
realize before now how hard that is for you. You are my heroes.*

My other heroes are our friends and family who've selflessly walked this road with us. Your support...means so so much. I am humbled by your love and thoughtfulness. The journey isn't over, but the outlook is fantastic because of a Good Father.

There is an ugly side to chemo and radiation, most of which is too personal to talk about. But there's also a beautiful side. One filled with things like love, joy, gratitude, and peace. Things that can only come from the presence of God. I haven't even begun to process most of these things yet, so today I'm going to start with something simple.

I'm going to appreciate my trip to Walmart, and I will not complain about going, ever again. Feel free to hold me accountable for that.[32]

This book's release marks three years from the day I heard the word *cancer*. My mind and heart are brimming with so much more to share. Just like the potential we found in Acacia Grove near the Jordan River, a lot has happened on the journey. So with all the possible ways we could wrap up our time together, why would I choose to begin this final and most important chapter with a passing thought about a trip to buy groceries? Because in the short time span between writing that post and right now, I caught myself complaining about going to Walmart.

Again.

Which brings up an important question to consider: How could I stumble back into the same habits so easily? How could I falter in my trust walk after all I've been through? Thinking back on my conversations with God about Rahab, I wouldn't have believed it either. But then, I got it. (I've grown to love God's little reality checks.) You see, the unraveled me would've condemned myself for staying tied to old habits. She would've chastised herself for her faults and questioned her ability to trust in God without wavering. She may have even become totally undone and fallen back into her old habits.

The *new me* understood I had made progress, and progress always gives us reason to rejoice. So let me encourage you with this. Each small step is progress, soul-sister.

Here's the deal. I don't want you to think I have it all figured out. This whole trusting thing is a process. One we will continue *building on* and *dwelling in* until the day we wrap our arms around Jesus' neck and soak in all his lasting glory. We will have setbacks in our quest to trust God more, but we've experienced incredible growth, releasing worry to secure daily peace and joy. Imagine me clapping loud enough for everyone to hear and maybe even embarrassing myself a little as I cheer us on. This is definitely a victory, my friend!

I believe as we give things to God, He in turn wants us to develop the wisdom and gumption to do what He calls us to do. When we see the result of our obedience, we can be proud of the work we've done in our spiritual journey. I hesitated before writing the word *proud* here. We're taught as Christian women to guard against pridefulness. We should remain humble and meek, and all those good things. But I think in this case, it's warranted. So I'm going to say it right here, right now. (Acknowledging that we couldn't have done it on our own.)

I'm proud of us!

I had many opportunities in this journey of trust to return to that 3-ring binder from not-so-long-ago and let the temptation of the envelope lure me back to my pattern of worry, doubt, and defeat. You had those choices too. We all did. And instead, we chose to shut the gate. To cinch our rope. To build a strong shelter with God's undeniable Word. And to keep Him at the center of it all.

An Unbreakable Cord

By now we've grown close, you and me. You've seen that even though I waited to open my envelope until the worst was in the past, God revealed what I needed to know when I needed it. The decision to trust Him helped me walk in steadfast resolve rather than entertaining defeating thoughts. Sure, there were times when fear of the worst-case scenario grabbed hold. When I didn't react the way I should. When I wanted to scream and cry and admit my fear that it wouldn't be okay! But then I'd remember our first foundation principle, seeing the change in me and admitting I needed God's help. And you know what? After that milestone trip to Walmart, I *did* open that envelope. I read the words that certainly would've rocked me to the core just a few months before. Only—in that moment—something unexpected happened. *Something remarkably unexpected.* Yes, God had healed me from a devastating and potentially fatal disease, but that was only a piece of the miracle He wanted me to discover.

> *What we find in the process of trusting*
> is *the miracle, whether the promise*
> *unfolds the way we expect or not.*

"For the word of the Lord holds true, and we can trust everything he does" (PSALM 33:4 NLT).

As I reviewed the doctor's words scribbled in bold, black ink, I felt the Lord's peace. I had found the secret to living the abundant life God gives, whatever the future holds. To not be completely undone by life's hardest trials; and instead, cinching my trust to God's guarantee in all things, holding unwaveringly to His promises.

Before releasing this book into the world, I gathered a sweet group of women together to read it and give me their feedback. Their thoughts and ideas made this message the best it could be, and for that I am forever grateful. In one of her responses in the group, Nancy said it well, "A lot of us have many envelopes. To remember to step back rather than surge ahead is very important and impactful, as it gives the Holy Spirit time to 'talk' with us about how to handle the situation, and to remind us that He already has it."

The challenges we face will beckon us to tie our trust to unreliable things, opening the way for worry, indecision, and frustration to follow. Now we have what it takes to stare down our envelopes with resolve, accept peace come what may, and exude joy along the way.

1 Peter 4 ends with this powerful statement to encourage us in those times when we pray and pray but don't receive the answer we hoped for, "So if you are suffering in a manner that pleases God, keep on doing what is right, and trust your lives to the God who created you, for he will never fail you" (1 Peter 4:19 NLT). Woman of God, let's never stop believing in our Heavenly Father to provide a miracle, even if sometimes that miracle looks nothing like we thought. Learning to trust in a God who cannot

fail may not always change our circumstances, but it will change us. No doubt about it.

Lord, may we be able to see the miracle transformation you are working in and through us as we learn to trust you.

...To This Day

I couldn't close the window on our time together without letting you know how things turned out for Rahab. She is our woman of the hour, after all. We've grown close to her, understanding her motives and caring about her future. Like an afterword in a good story, we want to know how things ended for Rahab and her new Israelite tribe. The last we heard from her, she was living with the Israelites "to this day" (JOSHUA 6:25). By reading ahead in the book of Joshua, we might guess her journey ended there. A nice happily-ever-after tied up in a big red bow. But from the testimony in the book of Matthew several hundred years later, we are blessed with the rest of Rahab's story.

"Salmon was the father of Boaz (whose mother was Rahab). Boaz was the father of Obed (whose mother was Ruth). Obed was the father of Jesse. Jesse was the father of King David" (MATTHEW 1:5-6A NLT).

The lineage list continues in Matthew chapter one, where the birth of Jesus reveals Rahab's role and her connection to us today.

She married Salmon of the tribe of Judah and took her place as an ancestor of Jesus Christ, the Savior of the World. "Salmon was a prince of the house of Judah, and thus, Rahab, the one time heathen harlot, married into one of the leading families of Israel and became an ancestress of our Lord."[33]

Reading about Rahab's destiny fulfilled, we see the beauty of how God once again wove the never-ending story of his precious son Jesus throughout all of Scripture. The good news of our Savior was foretold by prophets like Isaiah in the Old Testament who proclaimed, "For to us a child is born, to us a son is given, and the government will be on his shoulders. And he will be called Wonderful Counselor, Mighty God, Everlasting Father, Prince of Peace" (ISAIAH 9:6 NIV).

So we would be remiss if we closed Rahab's chapter without mentioning the significance of the scarlet color of her rope. My friend Merry said it so well in our focus group, "Just as the red cord represented a binding oath between Rahab and God, for us today the red blood of our Lord Jesus Christ represents the sealed covenant between believers and God. When we accept what Christ has done for us we cinch the covenant."

Thank you, Jesus, for giving your life, shedding your blood, and saving us all.

God blessed Rahab beyond what she could imagine. The Israelites faced many more battles after that, and those battles surely brought more trials to Rahab's door. We may not have a record of her daily life in the years to come, but I choose to believe our bold friend in the faith continued walking in obedience. Trusting God. Recalling how her Lord saved her. And of course, remembering her red rope.

So as we close the gate on our time together (I'm feeling those tears welling up again), I'd like to leave us with one last thought for what lies ahead for each of us. Rahab's scarlet cord brings to mind a saying I've heard most of my life. Maybe you've heard it too; it goes something like this:

"When you reach the end of your rope, tie a knot and hang on." — Author unknown.

Now that we've decided to live in freedom, faith, and steadfast resolve, we can look at that phrase from a new perspective. We began this book together, unraveling at each unpredictable circumstance. Hanging on for dear life. Wishing things could be different and holding on to something elusive. But not anymore. We know the secret to victorious living. We have all the intel we need, and we plan to use it.

When we reach the end of our rope, we won't just tie it. We'll cinch it to God's promise. That cord we've been weaving together? It is strong and solid, sister.

Living with unwavering trust in our unfailing God *is* possible. I'm so thankful we've discovered this truth together. We are ready to demonstrate a level of trust that draws others to our Lord. And when we ask ourselves that question, "Do I live like I trust God?" The answer will be a resounding *yes*.

Glossary of God's Promises

An Alphabetical Topical List of Encouraging Verses from God's Word

ABUNDANT LIFE

- "He fills my life with good things. My youth is renewed like the eagle's!" PSALM 103:5 NLT

- "in that I command you today to love the Lord your God, to walk in His ways, and to keep His commandments, His statutes, and His judgments, that you may live and multiply; and the Lord your God will bless you in the land which you go to possess." DEUTERONOMY 30:16 NLT

- "You can make this choice by loving the Lord your God, obeying him, and committing yourself firmly to him. This is the key to your life. And if you love and obey the Lord, you will live long in the land the Lord swore to give your ancestors Abraham, Isaac, and Jacob." DEUTERONOMY 30:20 NLT

- "Stay on the path that the LORD your God has commanded you to follow. Then you will live long and prosperous lives in the land you are about to enter and occupy." DEUTERONOMY 5:33 NLT

- "Take delight in the Lord, and he will give you your heart's desires." PSALM 37:4 NLT

- "The way of the godly leads to life; that path does not lead to death." PROVERBS 12:28 NLT

- "Fear of the Lord is a life-giving fountain; it offers escape from the snares of death." PROVERBS 14:27 NLT

- "You shall be blessed above all peoples. There shall not be male or female barren among you or among your livestock." DEUTERONOMY 7:14 ESV

- "The fear of the Lord prolongs life, but the years of the wicked will be short." PROVERBS 10:27 ESV

FORGIVENESS

- "He forgives all my sins and heals all my diseases." PSALM 103:3 NLT

- "He has removed our sins as far from us as the east is from the west." PSALM 103:12 NLT

- "Let the wicked change their ways and banish the very thought of doing wrong. Let them turn to the Lord that he may have mercy on them. Yes, turn to our God, for he will forgive generously." ISAIAH 55:7 NLT

- "But He was pierced for our rebellion, crushed for our sins. He was beaten so we could be whole. He was whipped so we could be healed." ISAIAH 53:5 NLT

GOD'S PRESENCE

- "The Lord of hosts is with us; The God of Jacob is our refuge." PSALM 46:7 NKJV

- When they call on me, I will answer; I will be with them in trouble. I will rescue and honor them." PSALM 91:15 NLT

- "You make known to me the path of life; in your presence there is fullness of joy; at your right hand are pleasures forevermore." PSALM 16:11 ESV

GUIDANCE/FUTURE

- "For this God is our God for ever and ever; he will be our guide even to the end." Psalm 48:14 NIV

- "Put your hope in the Lord. Travel steadily along his path. He will honor you by giving you the land. You will see the wicked destroyed." Psalm 37:34 NLT

- "I will instruct you and teach you in the way you should go; I will counsel you with my loving eye on you." Psalm 32:8 NIV

- "And blessed is she who believed that there would be a fulfillment of what was spoken to her from the Lord." Luke 1:45 ESV

- "Lord, you alone are my inheritance, my cup of blessing. You guard all that is mine." Psalm 16:5 NLT

HEALING/HEALTH

- "I will not die; instead, I will live to tell what the Lord has done." Psalm 118:17 NLT

- "Beloved, I pray that you may prosper in all things and be in health, just as your soul prospers." 3 John 1:2 NKJV

- "He sent out his word and healed them; he rescued them from the grave." Jeremiah 30:17 NIV, Psalm 107:20 NIV

- "Then you will have healing for your body and strength for your bones." Proverbs 3:8 NLT

- "My child, pay attention to what I say. Listen carefully to my words. Don't lose sight of them. Let them penetrate deep into your heart, for they bring life to those who find them, and healing to their whole body." Proverbs 4:20-22 NLT

- "Suddenly, a man with leprosy approached him and knelt before him. 'Lord,' the man said, 'if you are willing, you can heal me and make me clean.' Jesus reached out and touched him. 'I am willing,' he said. 'Be healed!' And instantly the leprosy disappeared." MATTHEW 8:2-3 NLT

- "...By his wounds you have been healed." 1 PETER 2:24B NLT

- "But for you who fear my name, the sun of righteousness shall rise with healing in its wings. You shall go out leaping like calves from the stall." MALACHI 4:2 ESV

HELP

- "Commit everything you do to the Lord. Trust him, and he will help you." PSALM 37:5 NLT

- "I wait quietly before God, for my victory comes from him." PSALM 62:1 NLT

- "The Lord will fight for you; you need only to be still." EXODUS 14:14 NIV

- "Again I say to you, if two of you agree on earth about anything they ask, it will be done for them by my Father in heaven." MATTHEW 18:19 ESV

- "You who fear the Lord, trust in the Lord! He is their help and their shield." PSALM 115:11 ESV

- "The righteous person faces many troubles, but the Lord comes to the rescue each time." PSALM 34:19 NLT

■ "Make thankfulness your sacrifice to God, and keep the vows you made to the Most High. Then call on me when you are in trouble, and I will rescue you, and you will give me glory." PSALM 50:14-15 NLT

HOPE

■ "And he who was seated on the throne said, 'Behold, I am making all things new.' Also he said, 'Write this down, for these words are trustworthy and true.'" REVELATION 21:5 ESV

■ "Behold, I am doing a new thing; now it springs forth, do you not perceive it? I will make a way in the wilderness and rivers in the desert." ISAIAH 43:19 ESV

■ "We give thanks to you, O God; we give thanks, for your name is near." PSALM 75:1A ESV

■ "I pray that the eyes of your heart may be enlightened in order that you may know the hope to which he has called you, the riches of his glorious inheritance in his holy people," EPHESIANS 1:18 NIV

■ "I remain confident of this: I will see the goodness of the Lord in the land of the living." PSALM 27:13 NIV

LOVE

■ "Yet I still dare to hope when I remember this: The faithful love of the Lord never ends! His mercies never cease." LAMENTATIONS 3:21-22 NLT

■ "The Lord is merciful and gracious, slow to anger and abounding in steadfast love." PSALM 103:8 ESV

- "But the steadfast love of the Lord is from everlasting to everlasting on those who fear him, and his righteousness to children's children," PSALM 103:17 NLT

MERCY

- "Great is his faithfulness; his mercies begin afresh each morning. I say to myself, "The Lord is my inheritance; therefore, I will hope in him!" LAMENTATIONS 3:23-24 NLT

- "Therefore the Lord waits to be gracious to you, and therefore he exalts himself to show mercy to you. For the Lord is a God of justice; blessed are all those who wait for him." ISAIAH 30:18 ESV

- "People who conceal their sins will not prosper, but if they confess and turn from them, they will receive mercy." PROVERBS 28:13 NLT

- "The Lord has heard my cry for mercy; the Lord accepts my prayer." PSALM 6:9 NIV

PEACE

- "You keep him in perfect peace whose mind is stayed on you, because he trusts in you." ISAIAH 26:3 ESV

- "The mind governed by the flesh is death, but the mind governed by the Spirit is life and peace." ROMANS 8:6 NIV

- "I have said these things to you, that in me you may have peace. In the world you will have tribulation. But take heart; I have overcome the world." JOHN 16:33 ESV

PLANS

- "But for those who are righteous, the way is not steep and rough. You are a God who does what is right, and you smooth out the path ahead of them." ISAIAH 26:7 NLT

- "You will also declare a thing, And it will be established for you;" JOB 22:28A NKJV

- "Today I have given you the choice between life and death, between blessings and curses. Now I call on heaven and earth to witness the choice you make. Oh, that you would choose life, so that you and your descendants might live!" DEUTERONOMY 30:19 NLT

- "And the Lord said, 'That's right, and it means that I am watching, and I will certainly carry out all my plans.'" JEREMIAH 1:12 NLT

- "And we know that in all things God works for the good of those who love him, who have been called according to his purpose." ROMANS 8:28 NIV

- "'For I know the plans I have for you,' declares the Lord, 'plans to prosper you and not to harm you, plans to give you hope and a future.'" JEREMIAH 29:11 NIV

PROTECTION

- "Trust in the Lord and do good. Then you will live safely in the land and prosper." PSALM 37:3 NLT

- "He alone is my rock and my salvation, my fortress where I will never be shaken." PSALM 62:2 NLT

- "Because you have made the Lord your dwelling place—the Most High, who is my refuge—no evil shall be allowed to befall you, no plague come near your tent." PSALM 91:9-10 ESV

- "The Lord protects those of childlike faith; I was facing death and He saved me." PSALM 116:6 NLT

- "Those who fear the Lord are secure; He will be a refuge for their children." PROVERBS 14:26 NLT

- The Lord says, "I will rescue those who love me. I will protect those who trust in my name." PSALM 91:14 NLT

- "When the earth quakes and its people live in turmoil, I am the one who keeps its foundations firm." PSALM 75:3 NLT

PROVISION

- "And this same God who takes care of me will supply all your needs from his glorious riches, which have been given to us in Christ Jesus." PHILIPPIANS 4:19 NLT

- "You must serve only the Lord your God. If you do, I will bless you with food and water, and I will protect you from illness." EXODUS 23:25 NLT

- "And we are confident that he hears us whenever we ask for anything that pleases him. And since we know he hears us when we make our requests, we also know that he will give us what we ask for." 1 JOHN 5:14-15 NLT

- "I tell you, you can pray for anything, and if you believe that you've received it, it will be yours." MARK 11:24 NLT

REST/CALM

- "It is useless for you to work so hard from early morning until late at night, anxiously working for food to eat; for God gives rest to his loved ones." Psalm 127:2 NLT

- "For the Lord your God is living among you. He is a mighty savior. He will take delight in you with gladness. With his love, he will calm all your fears. He will rejoice over you with joyful songs." Zephaniah 3:17 NLT

- "Come to me, all who labor and are heavy laden, and I will give you rest. Take my yoke upon you, and learn from me, for I am gentle and lowly in heart, and you will find rest for your souls. For my yoke is easy, and my burden is light." Matthew 11:28-30 ESV

- "And he said, 'My presence will go with you, and I will give you rest.'" Exodus 33:14 NLT

- "Be still, and know that I am God. I will be exalted among the nations, I will be exalted in the earth!" Psalm 46:10 ESV

RESTORATION

- "O LORD my God, I cried to you for help, and you restored my health." Psalm 30:2 NLT

- "And the God of all grace, who called you to his eternal glory in Christ, after you have suffered a little while, will himself restore you and make you strong, firm and steadfast." 1 Peter 5:10 NIV

- "For I will restore health to you and heal you of your wounds, says the Lord." Jeremiah 30:17a NKJV

SALVATION/ETERNAL LIFE

- "Our God is the God of salvation; And to God the Lord belong escapes from death." PSALM 68:20 NKJV

- "I will reward them with a long life and give them my salvation." PSALM 91:16 NLT

- "He redeems me from death and crowns me with love and tender mercies." PSALM 103:4 NLT

- "And because you belong to him, the power of the life-giving Spirit has freed you from the power of sin that leads to death." ROMANS 8:2 NLT

- He himself bore our sins in his body on the tree, that we might die to sin and live to righteousness…" 1 PETER 2:24A NLT

STRENGTH/CONFIDENCE

- "My soul clings to you; your right hand upholds me." PSALM 63:8 NIV

- "Don't be afraid, for I am with you. Don't be discouraged, for I am your God. I will strengthen you and help you. I will hold you up with my victorious right hand." ISAIAH 41:10 NLT

- "Therefore, put on every piece of God's armor so you will be able to resist the enemy in the time of evil. Then after the battle you will still be standing firm." EPHESIANS 6:13 NLT

- "I can do all things through Christ who strengthens me." PHILIPPIANS 4:13 NKJV

- "God is our refuge and strength, A very present help in trouble." PSALM 46:1 NKJV

WORRY/STRESS

- "Let us hold unswervingly to the hope we profess, for he who promised is faithful." HEBREWS 10:23 NIV

- "Cast your cares on the Lord and he will sustain you; he will never let the righteous be shaken." PSALM 55:22 NIV

- "In the multitude of my anxieties within me, Your comforts delight my soul." PSALM 94:19 NKJV

- "Don't worry about anything; instead, pray about everything. Tell God what you need, and thank him for all he has done. Then you will experience God's peace, which exceeds anything we can understand. His peace will guard your hearts and minds as you live in Christ Jesus." PHILIPPIANS 4:6-7 NLT

GENERAL ENCOURAGEMENT

- "For the Lord God is a sun and shield; the Lord bestows favor and honor. No good thing does he withhold from those who walk uprightly." PSALM 84:11 ESV

- "Let all that I am praise the Lord; may I never forget the good things he does for me." PSALM 103:2 NLT

- "The Lord gives righteousness and justice to all who are treated unfairly." PSALM 103:6 NLT

- "And Jesus answered them, 'Truly, I say to you, if you have faith and do not doubt, you will not only do what has been done to the fig tree, but even if you say to this mountain, 'Be taken up and thrown into the sea,' it will happen.'" MATTHEW 21:21 ESV

- "He was fully convinced that God is able to do whatever he promises." ROMANS 4:21 NLT

- "And if you are Christ's, then you are Abraham's offspring, heirs according to promise." GALATIANS 3:29 ESV

- "For God has not given us a spirit of fear and timidity, but of power, love, and self-discipline." 2 TIMOTHY 1:7 NLT

- "What then shall we say to these things? If God is for us, who can be against us?" ROMANS 8:31 ESV

- "Now to him who is able to do far more abundantly than all that we ask or think, according to the power at work within us," EPHESIANS 3:20 ESV

- "The Lord is close to the brokenhearted; he rescues those whose spirits are crushed." PSALM 34:18 NLT

Many Thanks!

This book wouldn't have happened without the support of some incredible people. God gave me the peace, resolve, and strength to share from my vulnerable places. I praise Him for this work He allowed me to be a part of. All glory belongs to my Heavenly Father for the message of this book.

Phil, I would not be here today if it were not for you— the patient, kind, and caring man God gave me. Thank you honey, for putting my needs ahead of your own, always. (And for making me scrambled eggs with cheese when I couldn't keep anything else down.)

Mom, you are no doubt my biggest encourager. Thank you for driving back and forth hundreds of times to help out, offer comfort, and give me much-needed distractions from the pain. Our relationship is truly special, and I am grateful for that.

My family, you are my reason for being. If there's one thing this journey of trust has taught me, it's that I need to tell you this more often. I love you more than words can say.

My church family, what an awesome example of walking in faith and trusting God you are! You uplifted me in my darkest days and prayed me through with assurance that we would see God's goodness in the land of the living. I am thankful for each one of you.

To my friends who allowed me time to process in the stillness and stuck around when I was ready to talk about my trial. Thank you just doesn't seem like enough. I appreciate you.

Bloggers Unite crew, we have something special. I love that we walk alongside each other, offering advice, prayer support, and friendship. Thank you.

The Cinched Focus Group, what can I possibly say to express my gratitude? You gave your time, thoughts, ideas, and more. Because of you, this book is better than I ever hoped it could be. And a special helping of gratitude to the brave people who allowed me to share your stories. I am honored.

And finally, to you. My soul-sister *Cinched* reader. I'm beyond glad you joined me in finding the level of trust we both knew was possible. Thanks for the laughs and tears, too. I pray you've learned as much as I have. You are a blessing to me.

Endnotes

CHAPTER 1

1. Heb. 11:31 NLT

2. Kadari, Tamar. "Rahab: Midrash and Aggadah." Jewish Women: A Comprehensive Historical Encyclopedia. 31 December 1999. Jewish Women's Archive. (Viewed on June 30, 2021) <*https://jwa.org/encyclopedia/article/rahab-midrash-and-aggadah*>.

3. Ruth 2:2

4. "Topical Bible: Cord," *Smith's Bible Dictionary*. Accessed March 30, 2020. *https://biblehub.com/topical/c/cord.htm*

5. Easton, M.G. "Cord," *Easton's Bible Dictionary*. Accessed March 30, 2020. *Bible Study Tools. https://www.biblestudytools.com/dictionaries/eastons-bible-dictionary/cord.html*

CHAPTER 2

6. Barker, Kenneth. "Joshua 2:1." *Expositor's Bible Commentary, (Abridged Edition): Old Testament.* Accessed April 2, 2020. *www.biblegateway.com*

7. Henry, Matthew. "Joshua 2:1." *Matthew Henry's Commentary.* Accessed April 2, 2020. *www.biblegateway.com*

8. Brown, Kristine. "A Week of Prayers for Hearing from God." August 2, 2020. *https://www.ibelieve.com/faith/week-of-prayers-for-hearing-from-god.html*

CHAPTER 3

9. Joy, Arabah. *Trust without Borders* (Published by Arabah Joy, 2014), Chap. 3, Kindle, e-book location: 386

10. Wilson, Debbie. *Little Women Big God*, (Abilene, Texas: Leafwood Publishers, 2016) pg. 46.

CHAPTER 4

11. Jennifer Powell Mundine, July 28, 2019. Facebook

12. Barker. "Proverbs 29:25." *Expositor's Bible Commentary, (Abridged Edition): Old Testament.* Accessed June 26, 2020. *www.biblegateway.com*

CHAPTER 5

13. Fletcher, Elizabeth. "Houses, tents, housing in ancient Bible times." Accessed August 3, 2020. *https://www.womeninthebible.net/bible-archaeology/ancient_houses/*

14. McDonald, Abby. "Why We Can Give the Unknown to God." January 23, 2020. *https://abbymcdonald.org/2020/01/give-the-unknown-to-god/*

15. Josh. 2:16 AMP. "And she said to them, 'Go [west] to the hill country, so that the pursuers [who have headed east] will not encounter you; hide yourselves there for three days until the pursuers return. Then afterward you can go your way.'"

16. William MacDonald and Arthur Farstad. "Joshua 2:1-24." *Believer's Bible Commentary*. Accessed August 3, 2020. *www.biblegateway.com*

17. Evans Shepherd, Linda. *When You Need to Move a Mountain*, (Grand Rapids, MI: Baker Group, 2019) pg. 67.

18. "Tiqvah," *Bible Hub*. Accessed August 3, 2020. *https://biblehub.com/hebrew/8615.htm*

CHAPTER 6

19. Elwell, Walter. *Evangelical Dictionary of Biblical Theology (Baker Reference Library)* Accessed August 3, 2020. *https://www.biblestudytools.com/dictionary/seal/*

20. Maddox, Micah. *Anchored In*, (Nashville, TX: Abingdon, 2017) pg. 41

CHAPTER 7

21. Guzik, David. "Joshua 5 – Circumcision and Passover at Gilgal." Accessed November 30. 2020. *https://enduringword.com/bible-commentary/joshua-5/*

22. Josh. 5:10 NLT

CHAPTER 8

23. Frost, Robert. "The Road Not Taken." *Atlantic Monthly*, 1915.

24. Shirey, Kathryn. "7 Keys to Trusting God's Plan for Your Life" August 28, 2019. *https://www.prayerandpossibilities.com/7-truths-about-trusting-gods-plan-for-your-life/*

CHAPTER 9

25. "The Walls of Jericho" Associates for Biblical Research. Accessed November 30, 2020. *https://www.biblestudytools.com/blogs/associates-for-biblical-research/the-walls-of-jericho.html*

26. "The Walls of Jericho" Associates for Biblical Research. Accessed November 30, 2020. *https://www.biblestudytools.com/blogs/associates-for-biblical-research/the-walls-of-jericho.html*

27. Brown, Kristine. "How to Follow God's Plan." July 18, 2018. *https://www.crosswalk.com/faith/spiritual-life/how-to-follow-god-s-plan.html*

CHAPTER 10

28. Dunham, Duwayne, director. 1993. *Homeward Bound: The Incredible Journey.* Walt Disney Pictures

29. De Cruz, Betsy. *More of God: A Distracted Woman's Guide to More Meaningful Quiet Times,* (Self-published by Betsy De Cruz: 2019) pg. 13.

30. Bengston, Michelle. *Breaking Anxiety's Grip* (Grand Rapids, MI: Baker Group, 2019) pg. 41.

31. Mullins, Jonita. "September newsletter." September, 2020. *www.okieheritage.com*

CHAPTER 11

32. Kristine Brown. February 11, 2019. Facebook

33. Lockyer, Herbert. *Lockyer's All the Women of the Bible - Rahab* (Zondervan, 2019) Accessed April 12, 2021. *www.biblegateway.com*

KristineBrown.net

CinchedBook.com

About the Author

Kristine Brown is a communicator at heart, nurturer by God's design, and life-long learner and teacher. She is a wife, mom, stepmom, and Mimi.

Kristine and her husband have endured challenges like infertility, long-distance family relationships, life-threatening illness, and life in ministry. Through it all, Kristine has seen God's faithfulness and felt His unfailing love. One of her favorite things is connecting women today with women of the Bible through our mutual experiences.

Kristine is a contributing writer for *iBelieve.com*, *Crosswalk.com*, Unlocked for Teens devotions, and more. You'll also find her work published on P31's Encouragement for Today, Christianity Today, and (in)Courage. She and her husband Phil live in Texas.

To connect with Kristine or learn more about her other books and resources, visit her online home, *www.kristinebrown.net.*

Printed in the USA
CPSIA information can be obtained
at www.ICGtesting.com
LVHW021549060923
757325LV00018B/160